THIS INCREDIBLY BENEVOLENT FORCE

This Incredibly Benevolent Force

*The Holy Spirit in Reformed Theology
and Spirituality*

Cornelis van der Kooi

William B. Eerdmans Publishing Company
Grand Rapids, Michigan

Wm. B. Eerdmans Publishing Co.
4035 Park East Court SE, Grand Rapids, MI 49546
www.eerdmans.com

© 2018 Cornelis van der Kooi
All rights reserved

Hardcover edition 2018
Paperback edition 2021

ISBN 978-0-8028-8241-7

Library of Congress Cataloging-in-Publication Data

Names: Kooi, Cornelis van der, author.
Title: This incredibly benevolent force : the Holy Spirit in reformed
   theology and spirituality / Cornelis van der Kooi.
Description: Grand Rapids, Michigan : William B. Eerdmans
   Publishing Company, [2018] | Includes bibliographical references
   and index.
Identifiers: LCCN 2017031273 | ISBN 9780802882417 (pbk. : alk. paper)
Subjects: LCSH: Holy Spirit. | Reformed Church—Doctrines. |
   Spirituality—Reformed Church.
Classification: LCC BT121.3 .K66 2018 | DDC 231/.3—dc23
LC record available at https://lccn.loc.gov/2017031273

Unless otherwise noted, Scripture quotations are from the New Revised
Standard Version of the Bible, copyright © 1989 by the Division of Christian Education of the National Council of the Churches of Christ in the
U.S.A., and used by permission.

Amatissimae sociae vitae,
Margriet

Contents

Foreword by Daniel Castelo	ix
Preface	xiii
Abbreviations	xvii
1. The Promise of Pneumatology *Cosmological Emptiness and the Spirit of God*	1
2. The Identity of Christ *Logos and Spirit*	22
3. The Anointed Son *Toward a Sustainable Spirit-Christology*	46
4. God's Spirit as Transformative Power *Voices from the Reformed Tradition*	71
5. The Threefold Office *Criterion for Living the Christian Life*	99
6. Eyes and Ears Open to the World *Discernment and Hope*	124

CONTENTS

Bibliography	144
Index of Authors	150
Index of Subjects	153
Index of Scripture References	156

Foreword

This collection of lectures represents a delightful exercise in pneumatological reflection. I say "delightful" in part because it occasions a kind of joy, not simply because of its subject matter, but also because of its style and approach. This little work represents a "new moment" on a number of levels. Let me elucidate.

First, this work is grounded and written out of a self-identified location, namely the Reformed tradition. For some reason, my impression is that this kind of self-identification within theological endeavoring is scarce, perhaps because it sounds like a kind of ecclesial parochialism. If this impression is true, it is unfortunate. Many will accommodate the particularity of "story" and "narrative" in various mediums, including entertainment, teaching, and even preaching, but the appeal of a kind of universalism or of a species of ecclesial agnosticism is still quite strong in sectors of the theological academy. Capitulation to this appeal is unfortunate because theologians and their works come from somewhere; inevitably, theological reflection is grounded in something culturally, socially, communally. The point is obvious, of course, yet repeatedly ignored, especially in systematic theology and dogmatics. To pretend that theological reflection is otherwise is to accept and promote a kind of willful ignorance, one that gets in the way time and time again in the appropriation and execution of theological reasoning. I am grateful that Van der Kooi identifies himself as part of and engaging with a theological and cultural tradition. This is an honest approach. It is theologically appropriate. In fact, I would say it is much needed.

Second, this work stems from and is aimed at its location in an engaging and spacious way. Van der Kooi treats of the Reformed tradition in a praiseworthy manner. He lifts up notable features of the tradition, including cherished characteristics and hallmarks, but he is also willing to admit some of its limitations. That kind of critical engagement is noteworthy, again, because of its relative scarcity. Being faithful to a tradition involves, in part, accounting for its shortcomings, and this for its own good. This kind of work can also be for the good of the Christian whole since such a recognition opens the possibility for charitable ecumenical and intercultural exchange. So, for instance, Van der Kooi as a Reformed theologian can speak of things that the Reformed tradition can learn from Pentecostal and charismatic groups. He also speaks of developments and contributions from the global South, a reality that represents the present and future of much of global Christianity. His self-location need not mean some kind of exclusive self-privileging. Rather, it represents a kind of transparency that can be the foundation for genuine engagement and exchange. One sees this foundation at work as he stresses the complementarity of theological models in certain cases as well as resists abstraction on particular points.

Foreword

Finally, this work energetically points to possibility, which is always wonderful to see in a volume on the Holy Spirit. Van der Kooi considers a number of themes, not necessarily exhaustively but provocatively so as to broaden readers' imaginations, to get them thinking in new ways. Approaches to Spirit Christology, the role of practices in dogmatics, the ministry of healing, anointing, and liberation in spirituality—these are simply some of the talking points he raises that have the potential to inspire and to challenge. In the work, Van der Kooi introduces the metaphor of unused wiring within a home for an electrical socket as illustrative of the untapped potential for thinking of anointing in terms of Calvin's threefold office of Christ; the metaphor can also be applied to pneumatology more generally in our current situation. It is quite obvious that Van der Kooi believes the work of the Spirit has the potential to change and transform reality here and now. Such an approach is refreshing and vitalizing.

My desire for this delightful book is that it can serve the Spirit's purposes of renewal, healing, and empowerment in the church and world today.

DANIEL CASTELO
Professor of Dogmatic and
Constructive Theology
Seattle Pacific University
and Seminary

Preface

This book contains the 2014 Annie Kinkead Warfield Lectures, which I was honored to deliver at Princeton Theological Seminary between March 31 and April 3. I would like to thank the trustees of this seminary, the faculty, and especially President Craig Barnes and my host, Bruce McCormack. It was a great privilege to reflect on the topic of the Holy Spirit in Reformed theology and spirituality at this great institution, which has been so important for the development of responsible theology for the church and the world. The choice of the topic was not random. Not only has pneumatology as an avenue into the whole of Christian doctrine and practice long attracted my own interest, but it was exactly half a century ago that Hendrikus Berkhof gave his Warfield Lectures on the very same topic. Whereas Berkhof could still say that pneumatology was a neglected field in systematic theology, fifty years later this statement can no longer be repeated. As will be shown in the following chapters, there are many good reasons to pick up the challenge to rethink Christian doctrine from the perspective of the work and person of the Holy Spirit. The role of the Holy Spirit has been addressed in the context of the ecumenical movement, plus deeper encounter with other religions has also been a reason for rethinking this topic. More important, however, has been the rise of the worldwide Pentecostal and charismatic movements and their influence in practices and rituals in many churches. Last but not least, I mention here the role that biblical theology has played during these years in reconsidering the relation of Christ and the Spirit. Spirit Christology has long had a bad name and been associated with liberal theology. In these chapters I explore a way in which the variety and multiplicity of the biblical data can give us good theological reason to allow an approach from multiple perspectives in which the role of the Holy Spirit is more emphasized than the older theology allowed.

Contemporary theological reflection, however, should not restrict itself to the relation of Christ and the Spirit. It is also a question of practical life whether we in our time see the benevolent work of that Spirit. It is a life question insofar as, more than ever, contemporary generations are aware of the vastness of our cosmic history and the mystery of life. The task of theology includes giving attention and orientation to the touch of the Spirit. These chapters are meant to serve such a goal. If Christ reigns and his Spirit has been sent, then this world is not empty but has become the space in which Christ by his Spirit works and manifests himself, especially against resistance, breakdown, and chaos. Reformed theology has historically featured the Spirit of God as having transformative power. In chapter 4 I explore this line of thought in the work of John Calvin, Friedrich Schleiermacher, and Abraham Kuyper. It challenges our way of assessing contemporary culture and society. In chapter 5 I address the relation between Christ and us by using a metaphor that shows up in the Heidelberg Catechism, one that is rarely noticed: the metaphor of anointing, a pneuma-metaphor. Perhaps we could use this tool to incorporate some insights from the Pentecostal movement and to further the conversation. Several dialogues between representatives from Presbyterian churches and from Pentecostal churches have been held. Despite much agreement, a difference has remained over the way Word and Spirit are related. Is the work of the Spirit fully dependent on the Word of God, or does this Spirit of Christ give people wisdom and prophetic insight about what in the name of God can now be said and done in our present context?

These chapters are exploratory; they do not give final answers. They invite readers to think for themselves, to criticize, and to continue the discussion about the role of the Holy Spirit within our theology and its Trinitarian framework. I am well aware that theological reflection is not a substitute for life itself, but at least it can be part of a life that takes up our responsibility for the time and place in which we live.

Abbreviations

CO	John Calvin, *Ioannis Calvini opera omnia quae supersunt*
Comm	*Communio*
Inst.	John Calvin, *Institutes of the Christian Religion*
TS	*Theological Studies*
VF	*Verkündigung und Forschung*

1 The Promise of Pneumatology
Cosmological Emptiness and the Spirit of God

The film *American Beauty* is a story about emptiness. The film describes two neighborhood middle-class families with beautiful homes on a quiet street, somewhere in an ordinary city. Under the surface of modern luxury, however, roils the struggle to give meaning to their lives. Each of the characters in the story illustrates the point that beauty is a sham—they all attempt in their own way to rise above the situation, but each comes to a destructive ending. The beauty in this film is not the beauty of the rose being grown by Anne—this rose has no scent. Rather, we get to see beauty through the lens of the boy next door, who is in the habit of filming everything on his video camera.

One day he allows the girl next door to look at one of his videos. In a lengthy shot we see only a plastic bag, picked up by the wind and blown high and low among the red autumn leaves. The moving and swirling of the bag is the beauty that suddenly, amid the foolishness and helplessness of the adults, appears as a gift that the boy and the girl can look at together in great delight. This image provides meaning and cohesion. In the words of the boy, Ricky: "This bag was just

... dancing with me ... like a little kid, begging me to play with it.... That's the day I realized that there was this entire life behind things and this incredibly benevolent force that wanted me to know there was no reason to be afraid ... ever." A breakthrough of beauty takes place in the midst of the emptiness, a power that presents itself as benevolent. What is that power? What is its secret? Can Christian theology say something about it?

Robert Johnston has interpreted this film against the backdrop of the book of Ecclesiastes.[1] The Preacher is surprised about the continuation of all things, their endless cycle, and the perpetual fretting of people, and he asks himself what the meaning of it all is. Still, this book of Scripture does not preach cynicism. In the midst of these great questions, the Preacher determines that it is a gift of God when one knows how to enjoy what God has given (Eccles. 9:7-9). The Preacher has no firm grip on life, no encompassing grasp of things, but he does have awareness of the surprise, the suddenly appearing light, the beauty that lifts the heart. In this life, God makes himself known and grants people his gifts. With those gifts, light shines on the continuation of generations and the fretting of humanity. The endlessness, the strangeness, and sometimes the atrocious cruelty of the cosmos appear in the light of God's gift.

The book of Ecclesiastes, with its melancholic insights, is a part of the canon of the Christian church. One can ask whether it is placed at the edge of the canon, or perhaps is not at home there, or whether to the contrary, because of its

1. Robert K. Johnston, *Useless Beauty: Ecclesiastes through the Lens of Contemporary Film* (Grand Rapids: Baker Academic, 2004), 57-72.

own perspective, it actually *is* at home there. It is a voice that may be heard in the Christian faith community, where it will find recognition. In some sense, this voice is also taken up by the apostle Paul when he speaks about the futility to which creation is subjected, and about creation's slavery to corruption (Rom. 8:20-21). But this interpretation at the same time portrays the tension between the various voices we already encounter in the Hebrew Bible itself and even more in the canon of the Christian church. Human history in the New Testament stands in the light of the appearing of Jesus Christ. In the words of the ancient hymn in 1 Timothy 3:16, a history of salvation has been put in motion in which the Spirit is the driving force; this history includes Christ justified and glorified, which is meant to become public for all powers, times, and nations. The space of the cosmos, of heaven and earth, has become the space where this message resounds into the most distant corners because it concerns everything and everyone. That is the bold claim, the trumpet blast. The next question is how God does all this and where he touches our lives and our world. Is the "incredibly benevolent force" that can be suddenly discovered actually related to Christ's Spirit? Expressed in theological terms: Is what is at stake here the relation between the Spirit and Christ—the intertwining of pneumatology and Christology? There has been much discussion about the work of the Spirit in the past century. Continued reflection is of the greatest significance both for the church and for the life of faith.

What is our existence on this planet all about? Are we not giving too much weight to the history of Israel and Jesus Christ if we look there for an answer to the question about the significance and sense of this universe? Briefly, it is nothing less than a provocation, for several reasons, of which I mention only two. It is, to start with, already a provocation in the light of the unfathomable suffering that people—women, children, and men—experience through hunger, wars, genocide, terrorism, and the abuse of people. Besides personal suffering, we could add our ongoing history, in which peoples and nations perform evil against one another. It is also a provocation in a cosmological sense. When the Christian church asserts that, in the history of a Jewish man, God acted in a manner that is decisive for all of creation, such a perspective is at odds with the dizzying and bewildering experience that a visit to a modern observatory can bring about.

A visit to the Griffith Observatory in Los Angeles or the planetarium in the Dutch village of Dwingeloo imprints on us for a brief time the awareness of our own insignificance and vulnerability. We are specks of dust in the universe, slight vibrations in an incomprehensibly long history. Cosmologists teach us that, according to the latest calculations, the cosmos came into being 13.8 billion years ago and that the sun will probably continue many more millions of years. The existence of the cosmos will far surpass our own lifespan. We might therefore be tempted to put down the pen, live as well as possible, pass the earth along to the next generation in as whole and usable condition as we can, and leave it at that.

This is not to say that our experience at the observatory raises no urgent existential questions. Who are we in this segment of the universe, and how is this small segment of human history related to the many billions of years in the cosmos wherein we exist? In comparison with the enormous number of years that cosmologists have calculated for the existence of the cosmos, as well as the unknown distances that

Cosmological Emptiness and the Spirit of God

are examined in this science, human existence on earth is no more than a pinpoint in the cosmos. What does the expectation of the coming kingdom as pictured in the Gospels mean in the light of these dizzying numbers? Can we continue to maintain that the history of Jesus Christ, the life of this Jewish man, is central in our faith? Here we see the scandal of the particularity that brings Christianity into an isolated position within the religions: this life, this story is decisive.[2] In him, so we assert, God comes to the world; his life and what is fulfilled and accomplished in that life are determinative for the future of humanity and the world.

The New Testament documents refer in this context to "revelation." The history of the world and of humanity is no longer a closed book, and the powers that rule are no longer a cause for wondering and bewilderment but are placed in a horizon that includes a beginning and an end. The Spirit who filled and directed the life of Jesus Christ and who was present at creation is also determinative for our life horizon. "But in accordance with his promise, we wait for new heavens and a new earth, where righteousness is at home" (2 Pet. 3:13). That expectation is typical for what is said about the Spirit in the New Testament, where the Spirit embodies the eschaton, the end-point, the completion, the renewal that is realized in Jesus. God's Spirit is the power—more than that, "the incredibly benevolent force"—that is at work in Jesus Christ as the *kyrios* and that made him rise from the dead in God's glory. This eschatological Spirit is, according to Paul, now also at work in the congregation as an advance or a down payment. I cite here a brief statement of J. P. Versteeg: "*Kyrios* and *pneuma*

---

2. Karl Barth, *Church Dogmatics* IV/3, 314.

both belong to the eschaton. It is that one eschaton that *is* realized in the exalted Christ as *kyrios* and *becomes* realized by the Spirit in the congregation."[3] Such is the faith and hope that determine the horizon of the gospel. The world and our cosmos are not alone by themselves but are the place where God in small, mysterious ways begins history, in which he wants us to be involved. He begins small in order to end great. That insight places our reality, personally and universally, in hopeful tension. This tension between beginning and completion, between God who works in our world through the Spirit and who wants us to come along, makes it essential to pay attention to the work of the Spirit.

The Rise of Pneumatology

In the past half-century many profound developments have taken place especially in the area of pneumatology. In his *Doctrine of the Holy Spirit*, the publication of his 1964 Warfield Lectures, Hendrikus Berkhof could still write: "It is true, beyond a doubt, that pneumatology is a neglected field of systematic development."[4] Later, after the model of Heidegger's word *Seinsvergessenheit* (forgetfulness of being), even the term *Geistvergessenheit* (forgetfulness of spirit) was coined. This word, however, certainly cannot be applied to the current situation. In recent decades countless proposals have

---

3. J. P. Versteeg, *Christus en de Geest: Een exegetisch onderzoek naar de verhouding van de opgestane Christus en de Geest van God volgens de brieven van Paulus* (Kampen: Kok, 1971), 337.

4. H. Berkhof, *The Doctrine of the Holy Spirit*, 2nd ed. (Richmond: John Knox, 1967), 10.

Cosmological Emptiness and the Spirit of God

been brought forward that seek to elaborate a doctrine of the Holy Spirit. In many theological concepts, pneumatology has become the common denominator on which the whole theological construction rests. In that case, one could speak of a broad pneuma-theology. As examples, we can count the work of Paul Tillich and Geoffrey Lampe, as well as Berkhof. From among the Dutch, I mention my teacher Jan Veenhof. From among the evangelicals I mention Clark Pinnock, and among Roman Catholics, Yves Congar, Karl Rahner, Hans Küng and his students, as well as Roger Haight and Kilian McDonnell.

What prompted this new interest? Consider five factors: (1) a general new interest in religious experience, spirituality, and pneumatology, (2) the retrieval of Trinitarian theology, (3) modern biblical research, (4) the Pentecostal and charismatic renewal movements, and (5) the ecumenical movement. Here I discuss all five briefly, and then in the remainder of this chapter I elaborate particularly on the function of biblical research and the impact of the Pentecostal and charismatic renewal movements.

Renewal of Interest in Religion and Spirituality

First, the prominence of a broad pneumatology signifies an enormous shift in relation to the previous theological trend. In the eighteenth century and still in the nineteenth century, belief in God as Creator was still a shared conviction of society and culture, and the doctrine of creation was the common denominator in theology. In the twentieth century, however, this basis in the concept of creation as the place where God can be identified fell away. Two world wars and the awareness that this world suffers from an excess of cruelty and evil brought a long tradition of creation-based theology to its end; a new focus was found in Christology. Jesus Christ is the place in world history that enables us to get the (right) view of God. Or more precisely, the question of where God is was now answered with reference to the crucified Christ. There, in the hiddenness of suffering and death, God reveals his face. In the meantime, we are already in the next phase of development, and Christology seems driven out of its place. The exclusive concentration on Christ prompted the question of whether God can be experienced as Spirit. Is the rest of reality empty, and are Jesus Christ and the church's witness to him the only answer to which Christian theology can point? In the present cultural fascination with experience, spirituality, and the pivotal role of the human subject, that question is answered in the negative, and theologians again reach back to the notion of a universally present god-awareness. This development is the first reason for the interest in pneumatology. This universe is not empty. It is the place where God by his Spirit moves, dwells, struggles, and interferes. Immediately I add that the Reformed tradition offers an important point of contact to this new interest, especially because the Reformed tradition is rooted in the broad catholic tradition. To give one example, under the rubric "common grace," the Reformed tradition, especially its neo-Calvinistic branch, offers points of contact that are open for pneumatological reinterpretation.

Retrieval of Trinitarian Theology

Second, the recent attention to pneumatology can be readily connected to a Trinitarian line of approach that has again become popular in contemporary theology. The Spirit signifies God's activity and experience in the present and is the most focused point of God's involvement with us. His involvement, however, is not of one kind but is multiplex and diverse. These qualifications can be well connected with Trinitarian theology as a broader framework of theology as a whole. The Spirit plays a fundamental role in creation, in the continuation of history, in the life of Jesus, at the completion of this creation, and in the inner life of God. The Spirit is the Spirit of the Son and of the Father. We could therefore speak of a Trinitarian pneumatology. In chapters 2 and 3 we will come back to this Trinitarian framework when discussing the possibility of a Spirit Christology.

The Role of the Spirit in the Old and New Testaments

As a third factor, I mention a new interest in the biblical data. I recognize this is not completely new. One may point to what Warfield wrote during his time on the role of the Spirit in the Old and New Testaments.[5] But the interest in the role of the Spirit is not a little stimulated by modern biblical-theological scholarship.[6] This scholarship has given us insight into the

---

5. B. B. Warfield, "The Spirit of God in the Old Testament" and "The Leading of the Spirit," in *Biblical and Theological Studies*, ed. Samuel S. Craig (Philadelphia: Presbyterian & Reformed, 1952), 127-56 and 543-59.

6. James D. G. Dunn, *Jesus and the Spirit: A Study of the Religious and Charismatic Experiences of Jesus and the First Christians as Reflected in the New Testament* (London: SCM, 1975) and *Christology in the Making: A New Testament Inquiry into the Origins of the Doctrine of the Incarnation*, 2nd ed. (London: SCM, 1989); Gordon D. Fee, *God's Empowering Presence: The Holy Spirit in the Letters of Paul*, 5th printing (Peabody, MA: Hendrickson, 2002); M. Welker, *God the Spirit* (Minneapolis: Fortress, 1994).

varied functions and presence of the Spirit within the Old Testament and New Testament writings and has become an important factor in the interest that has been attached to pneumatology.

We should not neglect discussing the role of the Spirit in the Old and New Testaments, and I now offer brief remarks. These characteristics will be expanded upon in the following chapters, and here I offer a preliminary taste.

The Spirit brings to life—this is the Spirit's first role. The broader background of all the meanings of the concept of Spirit can be found in the connection between life and breath. The Hebrew word *ruach* and the Greek word *pneuma* have a similar background. Never has the original association of breath been lost. Spirit is that by which someone is a living being. This aspect can be found in the Old Testament for what we would call natural life, as well as for history. God's Spirit is the driving power in history—that is, the power who brings to life but who also can bring to an end as God's judgment (Exod. 15:8-10; Job 26:12-13; 33:4; Ps. 18:5; Isa. 40:6-7, Gen. 6:3).

The Spirit is the power of liberation—this is the Spirit's second role. The Spirit empowers people such as the judges and King Saul (Judg. 3:10; 6:34; 11:29). A close connection between the Spirit of prophecy, justice, and politics can be found in the Old Testament—that is, the theme of liberation (1 Sam. 10:10-11; 19:23-24). This implies also that the Spirit can retreat and that his empowerment can come to an end (Judg. 16:20).

A third role needs to be mentioned: the Spirit is the Spirit of the eschaton, or fulfillment. This eschatological aspect shows up particularly in the later prophets like Isaiah and Ezekiel. In

Cosmological Emptiness and the Spirit of God

Ezekiel the prophet is taken away in the Spirit, who tells the prophet what has to be said (Ezek. 2:2; 3:14; 11:5). The Spirit is the Spirit of restoration. The people of Israel will be restored, and according to Isaiah, the Messiah will be anointed as the Servant of God with the Spirit, who distinguishes him as God's envoy in the time of final restoration and worldwide justice (Isa. 32:15-16; 34:16; 57:16). Ultimately, all people in Israel will become bearers of that Spirit (Isa. 59:21). In the New Testament, Jesus as the *kyrios* is anointed by this eschatological Spirit, and it is by this Spirit that Jesus, in his exaltation, ushers in the eschaton.

A fourth role shows up already in creation but remains true for the eschaton, namely, that *the Spirit sets free* and finally creates the human being as a subject. When God creates, he creates something that is not-God, which is particularly true for the human being. This being stands before God as an agent with freedom. This one is called to give answer, which applies also when God is all in all. Our subjectivity and personhood are results of that call. The Spirit does not dehumanize us but is the personalizing Spirit. In the eschatological fulfillment, there will be freedom to love and to attach to God as the eternal source of life. This whole scenario was already present and visible in the life of Jesus. Jesus let himself be determined by the love of God the Father. It is also a promise for all God's children. God in his Spirit comes near. God may dwell in his creation but is not part of it. Creation objectifies the notion of otherness as something that is not God, an otherness that in eternity is not taken away. Only the estrangement that is the result of a sinful world will be taken away.

A fifth element in the work of the Spirit, closely related to the former one, is that the Spirit gives space. God is *a granting God*. He opens new space and in fact makes something new.

The Spirit of God is the principle of novelty—creating something that was not there before. The Greek notion that the eternal and divine is unchangeable and that this attribute belongs to God's simplicity should not be assumed as biblical. In classical thought, nothing new can be supposed to come in God.[7] That is, God is determined by his simplicity (*simplex esse*), which is taken to mean that he is unchangeable, for any change would diminish his being. For example, Herman Bavinck writes that "no new plan ever arose in God. In God there was always one single immutable will."[8] Is this what Scripture teaches us when it speaks of the Spirit who will create something new? The God of the Bible, the Father of Jesus, distinguishes himself by making something new, finding new avenues—something that was not in the past and that is in favor of salvation—and bringing forward his benevolence. In the next chapter, we will focus on that place or that person where the Christian community is pointing to when it comes to the question of where that benevolence has already become concrete in our cosmic history, namely, the history and person of Jesus of Nazareth.

Pentecostal and Ecumenical Impulses

In addition to these (1) cultural, (2) theological, and (3) biblical factors for renewed awareness of the Spirit, several

---

7. "Ergo neque novum obiectum in Dei scientiam venit; nam existeret in Deo nova scientia," Cocceius quote cited in H. Heppe and E. Bizer, *Die Dogmatik der evangelisch-reformierten Kirche* (Neukirchen: Neukirchener Verlag, 1958), 62.

8. H. Bavinck, *God and Creation*, vol. 2 of *Reformed Dogmatics*, trans. John Vriend (Grand Rapids: Baker Academic, 2004), 154.

Cosmological Emptiness and the Spirit of God

historical circumstances have stimulated the attention to pneumatology, namely, the Pentecostal and charismatic renewal movements and the ecumenical movement. These are the fourth and fifth factors. In both, we are dealing with transnational movements that have more in common than is often assumed and that have shaped the current situation. The ecumenical movement began as a missionary movement that, in its dynamism, was and has been strongly influenced by pneumatological ideas. It is the Spirit who moves borders and peoples, ultimately bringing people together. The statement on unity of the Tenth Assembly of the World Council of Churches, in Busan in 2013, speaks volumes.[9] We see the same transnational, mission-oriented, and therefore centrifugal drive in the Pentecostal movement. The Pentecostal renewal not only brought about an enormous, worldwide spreading of Pentecostal Christianity but, since the 1960s, has greatly influenced other churches through the larger charismatic renewal. Here we think of the Roman Catholic Church and especially of several decrees and constitutions of the Second Vatican Council (1962–65), notably *Lumen gentium* and *Gaudium et Spes*. Compared with the First Vatican Council (1869–70), the Second devoted much more space to pneumatological elements in ecclesiology and the role of the laity. The Pentecostal revival of the early twentieth century, through the charismatic renewal, also exerted great influence on Protestantism. Confessional boundaries grew less significant. In many ways, an osmosis took place between

9. For the "Unity Statement," see https://www.oikoumene.org/en/resources/documents/assembly/2013-busan/adopted-documents-statements/unity-statement?set_language=en.

evangelicalism and the charismatic renewal, especially in the area of practices—such as changes in music and worship culture, anointing of the sick, a growing interest in spiritual formation, discernment, and last but not least, the ministry of healing. The theological implications and assumptions of these practices have often not been sufficiently clarified or studied. They are still under debate and often cause friction within churches and faith communities. For that very reason, continuing study and dialogue about practice and theology remain important. It is a reason for rejoicing that we are largely past the time when the charismatic renewal encounters resistance and aversion, although remnants of different sorts of theological aversion and even close-mindedness may remain. The report of the most recent Reformed-Pentecostal dialogue is a witness to this changed relationship.[10] Instead of focusing on differences, this report emphasizes points of agreement. Nevertheless, the challenge and the quest are not nearly complete. I thus briefly sketch the main challenge still facing Reformed theology and pneumatology.

It is determinative and decisive for spirituality and for theological reflection that, on the basis of the New Testament witness about the kingdom of God, salvation bestowed by Christ is to be understood *holistically*. Salvation is not limited to eternal redemption and security in God, but it thrusts itself in all different ways into this life as liberation, justification, and healing—that is, as the appearance of God's kingdom in all its dimensions. It is exactly the eschatological connota-

---

10. Report of the Reformed-Pentecostal Dialogue, "Experience in Christian Faith and Life: Worship, Discipleship, Discernment, Community, and Justice," *Reformed World* 63, no. 1 (March 2013): 2–44.

tions in the preaching and actions of Jesus that form an essential aspect of Pentecostal and charismatic renewal and that represent a challenge to classic Reformed theology and spirituality. The Reformed tradition focuses the work of the Spirit primarily on conversion and personal holiness,[11] typically treating the physical, communal, and societal connotations of God's justification as subtopics of the final consummation. This sharp separation is broken down in Pentecostal and charismatic practice.

The Azusa Street Revival, which broke out in 1906 in Los Angeles, California, provides a good example of Pentecostal practice. In this signal event, old boundaries of gender, class, and race were broken down. Women participated just as much as men, and poor and rich praised God together.[12] William Seymour, one of the prominent leaders of the revival, came from a former slave family. These notions of a liberating presence of God can lead to an outcome that affects the social, economic, political, and physical areas of life, with exact details dependent on the specific context and a variety of cultural and theological factors.[13]

Historically, the gap between Reformed and Pentecostal has been wide, though in recent decades some bridges have been built. Every context, every region is different, and most worldwide statements overreach. In the Netherlands, one no-

11. For a fine recent example, see Wim van Vlastuin, *Be Renewed: A Theology of Personal Renewal* (Göttingen: Vandenhoeck & Ruprecht, 2014).

12. Cecil M. Robeck Jr., *The Azusa Street Mission and Revival: The Birth of the Global Pentecostal Movement* (Nashville: Nelson, 2006).

13. See particularly the work of Walter J. Hollenweger—for example, his *The Pentecostals* (London: SCM, 1972) and *Pentecostalism: Origins and Developments Worldwide* (Peabody, MA: Hendrickson, 1997).

tices a change in musical traditions, new accents in the liturgy such as greater emphasis on praising God, and an openness to anointing those who are ill. Some places have seen a new, tentative openness to considering charismatic worship. But the theological resistance and puzzlement are not nearly over—neither from liberals nor from conservatives. As mentioned above, older Reformed theology applied the work of the Spirit especially, if not exclusively, to being born again, conversion, and renewal, or sanctification. There was hardly room for charismata, since, according to the influential voice of B. B. Warfield, they no longer occur—they have ceased.[14]

But even where today the notion of God's kingdom is acknowledged as a holistic idea, there is still immediate hesitation, for example, if it involves healing. The theologies of Jürgen Moltmann and Wolfhart Pannenberg are examples of this position. Both scholars defend the idea that the future is already present here, but instead of becoming concrete, they remain stuck in generalities, if not obfuscations. This leads to the larger question: In the context of the modern worldview, how far can Reformed and Lutheran theology go in giving place to experiences that are mostly derived from the Southern Hemisphere? We must admit that we badly need such experiences. They are concrete events that the current churches of the Majority World, often in marginal situations, have witnessed with their practices of glossolalia, xenolalia, prophecy, healing, and deliverance from evil spirits—experiences that can pose a challenge for "standard" theology. The

14. For an example, see Cephas N. Omenyo, *Pentecost outside Pentecostalism: A Study of the Development of Charismatic Renewal in the Mainline Churches in Ghana* (Zoetermeer: Boekencentrum, 2002).

things we're talking about here are not simply exceptional or unusual experiences of healing and liberation but also events from everyday life. If we do not meet God there, in everyday life, where will we ever meet him?

Renewal Movements and the Retrieval of Pneumatology

To what extent has Pentecostalism been welcomed into meaningful Christian theological reflection? The Roman Catholic Church, on the basis of its experience with renewal movements throughout the centuries, seems to have a head start. I have mentioned the new openness of the Second Vatican Council, and we could point to the ongoing Catholic-Reformed dialogue. But to what degree has progress been made within the Reformed or the larger Protestant community? The emphasis on God's hiddenness can become so overwhelming in Western theology that it often becomes in effect a theology of God's absence.[15] This theme stands in stark contrast with Pentecostal and charismatic spirituality, but to be honest, it is also in contradiction with some obvious directions of Reformed theology and spirituality.

In the charismatic renewal within the Protestant world, new emphasis is given to the presence of God in ordinary life. We have much to learn here, not the least from churches in the Southern Hemisphere. In encounters with those

15. Although this may link up with an element in Barth's theology, namely God's hiddenness, God's *Bereitschaft* (willingness) to reveal himself has become marginalized.

churches, it becomes very clear in what respects Reformed theology should reflect on its own theology and spirituality—for example, when it comes to the relation between faith and health.[16] The older Reformed theology formed its ideas about faith and health mostly within some concept of general grace or with the conceptual neo-Calvinistic framework of common grace. The theological toolbox of the mission workers was filled with the idea that advanced medical knowledge and medical skills are the result of God's common grace, which means that when someone is sick, one just goes to a medical doctor. That is how God cares for healing nowadays, and it should not be expected that a prayer for healing or laying on of hands would be profitable for your physical body. That view smacks of magic and will lead to superstition. Put differently, the more holistic view of life, in which one must take account of the existence of evil spirits and the meaning of dreams and visions, is not considered.

The Reformed theology of my roots is a theology that has been deeply stamped by modernity. For those of us living in a modern Western context, such a heritage is almost inevitable; today, however, it is no longer sufficient. Somehow we need to take seriously the experiences of Pentecostal and charismatic churches in the Southern Hemisphere, churches often suffering under intense persecution. One of the issues that surfaced in the aforementioned Pentecostal-Reformed dialogue was that of discernment, on which, despite common agreement reached on other subjects, no unity could be achieved.

---

16. Deborah van den Bosch-Heij, *Spirit and Healing in Africa: A Reformed Pneumatological Perspective* (Bloemfontein: Sun Media, 2012).

Theological Reflection: Four Key Functions

The importance of a renewed reflection on pneumatology is not restricted to only one field or locus of theology but has wider significance. It affects the way of doing theology as such, and it clarifies or specifies the functions of dogmatic theology. In short, it has methodological implications. Particularly this field of Christian practice and experience shows that there is not only a line from dogmatics to practice, but also a line from practice to dogmatics. We will have to learn this truth anew when we address questions regarding the work of the Spirit. We need to take seriously the experiences of Christians and churches in our own context, as well as of those on other continents and in culturally very different contexts. If God by his Spirit deeply permeates human reality, and if the Spirit is sensitive to context and works in a polyphonic manner, then the experience of churches and Christian faith communities worldwide can be regarded as legitimate arenas for contemporary theological reflection.

With training gained from studying concrete experiences in an ecumenical context, dogmatics can better execute its functions. Here I list four of these functions, believing that they illuminate the way forward for contemporary Reformed theology. Dogmatics has (1) a *descriptive* function; it expresses and explains the essential contours and elements of what the church has always believed and still believes. It is "making sense" of Christian faith. It also has (2) a *normative* function, by which what is accepted as normative teaching of the church functions as a corrective tool. This normative function is the best known, and it must be acknowledged that this function has made dogmatics a subject of ill fame. "Dogmatic" has become a loaded, pejorative word. It is a function, however, that cannot be ignored. (In chapter 6, in speaking of discernment, I revisit this function.)

Perhaps more challenging for dogmatics is its third function: (3) *explorative* with respect to new experiences. On the basis of John 16:13, church and theology must be open to new or deepened understandings of God's will provided by the Spirit through a variety of contexts, experiences, and realities. Exploration, however, should always be cautious. Development in pneumatology means that we can use less grand, general, and encompassing statements than the pneumatological concepts of some decades ago. That is, it should be a realistic theology.[17] In the exploration of new experiences and practices, the systematic theologian should cooperate with experts in other disciplines, for example, anthropology, psychology, and medical science. New life experiences, technical and medical advances, and the opportunities afforded by the Internet and modern media require theological reflection. What is the religious content and significance of all these new experiences, and how should Christian theology respond to them? To answer thoughtfully requires space and courage for exploration. By means of such learning, dogmatics can execute its exploring function.

The most interesting and, as to its public function, most challenging task of dogmatics in our times, however, is (4) to provide *orientation*. Dogmatic concepts can help interpret life, identify the traces of the Spirit of Christ, and encourage people and churches in making their choices and reflecting on their practices. For the pastorate and for the development of

17. Welker, *God the Spirit*, 46.

Christian ethics, this function is important, for it helps us to identify the proper understanding of theological concepts and ideas. The concepts and ideas are not the life of faith itself, but they form and order the content of this faith. The life of faith, however, the actual relation of God and human beings, is more than such ordering. This orienting function is similar to a hiking guide. It is not the hike itself; it is a guide that can sometimes help you avoid getting lost and let you know where you are. Particularly when we talk about ordinary life and the guidance of the Spirit in the life of believers, this quest for direction and orientation becomes important. (Again in chapter 6, when we address discernment, we return to this question.)

2 The Identity of Christ
Logos and Spirit

A Pneumatological Perspective?

The Christian faith points us to the figure of Jesus of Nazareth as the one in whom God decisively drew near to the world, both personally and salvifically. In the context of world history, such a statement strikes us as altogether counterintuitive. It meets with derision from yesterday's and today's wise men and idealists, from cynics like Celsus to the Hegelian David Friedrich Strauss, who was convinced that the divine spirit could never pour itself out in just one person. Such an idea was *welthistorischer Humbug*. After all, how could one man, the individual history of one human being, ever bear such a significance? How could his history interrupt our reality and create a new horizon of expectation? This is, however, the very thing Christian faith is claiming. At the beginning of the Gospel of Matthew this good news (*euangelion*) is summarized in one name: Immanuel, God with us (Matt. 1:23). These words contain the promise of the Christian faith, which may strike us as being somewhat grotesque: our existence, our present, and our future now take place within a new horizon. God has come near to us in Christ, decisively near. That is the new thing for us.

In the church's teaching, attempts have been made to grasp that discovery with a concept derived from the prologue to the Gospel of John. Christ is the Word who was with the Father, the Word made flesh. For this reason we speak of a Logos Christology. At the same time, in this gospel itself the concept of pneuma also clearly plays a role in describing what makes the appearance of Jesus so special. This word refers to breath, to movement, and to life. The Word is heard in the breath of the Spirit. In this chapter and the next, I explore how a Spirit Christology can contribute to our reflection on Immanuel—what it means that God is with us, us human beings living in this universe.

A pneumatological perspective on Jesus and his identity offers rich possibilities—I would even say richer possibilities than a Logos Christology does—for contemplating what is human, historical, and dynamic, in the process also giving us a good or better view of what makes Jesus's relationship to the divine so special. This is the short answer as to why there is so much interest in a Spirit Christology. According to the critics of a Logos Christology, the classic doctrine undermines the humanity of Jesus and even lends itself to a certain docetism. For if the eternal Logos, who always remains what he is, is the personifying center of Jesus Christ, one may be left with a humanity that seems altogether static in him. Historical development, Christ's growth, and his suffering on the cross become difficult to grasp within a Logos Christology. They can pertain only to his human nature, which must in turn be considered anhypostatically; that is, the human nature of Christ is not an already existing individual or an independent reality in itself. It is made personal only in hypostatic union with the Logos. It is very difficult nowadays, however, to explain this doctrine of an "impersonal" human nature, for the word "person" makes us think right away of a being with a consciousness and a will. If Jesus is said to have had an "impersonal" human nature, we may be left with the impression that he actually was not fully human after all. Furthermore, the miracle of the incarnation appears to be that of two static natures put together, while the real miracle—namely, that God is active in order to save us in the one Jesus—disappears from view.[1] A Spirit Christology, so it is claimed, offers better perspectives for doing justice to the person of Jesus and to his humanity.

Even if we leave aside for now the question of how fair this criticism really is, we must at any rate admit that the Spirit plays a fundamental role in the biblical witness. In the book of Acts, we in fact find a description of Jesus in which his uniqueness is described in terms of his empowerment, or anointing, by the Holy Spirit: "That message spread throughout Judea, beginning in Galilee after the baptism that John announced: how God anointed Jesus of Nazareth with the Holy Spirit and with power; how he went about doing good and healing all who were oppressed by the devil, for God was with him" (10:37-38). The presence of God with Jesus, his assault on sicknesses and on the evil powers, is in this text connected with Jesus's anointing, or baptism, with the Spirit. It is the Spirit of the end times, who, in the dynamic of these end times, manifests himself as the benevolent force

---

1. So A. Schlatter, *Das christliche Dogma* (Stuttgart: Calwer, 1923), 335-38.

Logos and Spirit

in the life of Jesus. In this text, the attention is on what Jesus undertook to do, on the way in which the signs of the kingdom of God became evident around him. His meaning is determined by what he did and by his being equipped with the Spirit of God.

Furthermore, the Synoptic Gospels report that, immediately following Jesus's baptism in the Jordan, after he had been baptized with the Spirit, Jesus was driven into the wilderness by this same Spirit and tempted there (Matt. 4:1; Mark 1:12; Luke 4:1-2). But how are we to actually conceive of his temptation? Can this account be taken seriously if the eternal Son is the personifying center in Jesus? Or did Jesus indeed have to discover his own calling and mission by a process that involved many twists and turns, doubts and silences? According to the Epistle to the Hebrews, that was indeed the case. Jesus had to learn obedience as Son in his suffering (Heb. 5:1-9), which points to a process of hunger, abandonment, waiting, and discovery. Jesus did not all of a sudden just have the discernment of the spirits but had to learn it. This experience brings him closer to us, and us to him.

Another passage also prominently displays this search and discovery. In it Jesus answers the question that John sent him from prison: "Are you the one who is to come, or are we to wait for another?" (Matt. 11:3). This is a dramatic question in many respects, since John's entire life-quest is in fact at stake. Is Jesus the expected Messiah or not? Jesus does not answer John directly but responds with words from the prophet Isaiah: "Go and tell John what you hear and see: the blind receive their sight, the lame walk, the lepers are cleansed, the deaf hear, the dead are raised, and the poor have good news brought to them" (vv. 4-5). These were the signs of the shalom that the prophet Isaiah had attributed to the Spirit of the eschaton, and now these things were happening around Jesus by virtue of the Spirit who rested upon him. Yet, their significance was never self-evident; people could remain blind to it. Faith and commitment were demanded from the onlookers. This very aspect, however, brings us closer to today's questions: What can we hope for? With what can we go on living?

This dynamic and the question of our own participation in this dynamic make a Spirit Christology altogether captivating, as well as highly important within a systematic-theological perspective. Not only do we once more face the question as to who Jesus is, but we can at the same time ask how we ourselves participate in it. The metaphor of an anointment with, or a pouring out of, the Spirit directly raises the question as to our participation. It raises the question of the church and of mission.

At this point we come to several methodological questions relating to Christology. In using "method" here, I mean the way we are given access to the secret of Jesus Christ. How do we approach the question of the identity of Jesus? What are the avenues?

Methodological Questions

An overview of Christology immediately raises a number of methodological issues, including the question of the starting point of Christology, the role of the creeds, the role of biblical scholarship, and the place of experience in the formulation of doctrine.

From Above or from Below?

A natural place to start would be with the well-known distinction between a Christology "from above" and one "from below." Although, following Pannenberg, we do indeed admit the fundamental nature of this distinction,[2] it still must be acknowledged that this spatial metaphor itself is not entirely clear. What does it mean? Does "from below" mean that we begin with the historical Jesus, that is, with what can be established using the tools of historical scholarship? In that case, we might as well admit right away that this road will never lead us to the "above." To put it in the words of Barth, it is like a "desperate attempt to raise water from a stagnant pond to [a height of 3,000 meters] by using a hand-pump."[3] That's never going to work. If methodologically one admits only the activity of human agents, one will never arrive "above," where God is. As to the words "from above," they are indeed clear in that they point us to a starting point in a theology of revelation. Yet, here too we encounter confusion. For what exactly would the "below" then be? A theology of revelation can also begin "from below," that is, from God's work in history, in the "economy" of his acts. A theology of the third article of

---

2. See W. Pannenberg, *Systematic Theology*, vol. 2 (Edinburgh: T&T Clark, 1994); B. Kamphuis, *Boven en beneden: Het uitgangspunt van de christologie en de problematiek van de openbaring nagegaan aan de hand van de ontwikkelingen bij Karl Barth, Dietrich Bonhoeffer en Wolfhart Pannenberg* (Kampen: Kok 1999).

3. K. Barth, "Die dogmatische Prinzipienlehre bei Wilhelm Herrmann" (1925), in *Vorträge und kleinere Arbeiten, 1922-1925*, ed. H. Finze (Zürich: TVZ, 1990), 595; the translation is from Berard L. Marthaler, *The Creed: The Apostolic Faith in Contemporary Theology* (Mystic, CT: Twenty-third Publications, 1987), 121.

the Creed in fact moves in that trajectory: what is specific to the Spirit is the very fact that he has been sent into our world and is active here.

The real distinction, therefore, is between theologies that begin with divine revelation and those that exclude the category of God's acts altogether. Working from a belief in divine revelation, we can therefore start below, that is, in history, in the economy of God's acts and in the life of Jesus. According to the Scriptures, the Spirit of God rested on Jesus. The pneumatological dimension in the life of Jesus invites us to ask what is going on "below." "Above" is discovered "below." We thus have a methodological reason to start our reflections on Jesus, on God, and on the fate of our universe from "below" in the story of Israel and of Jesus as part of this story. That story and his life and acts are the lens to get to know what is "above"—that is, the being of God.

The Creed as Starting Point

A second and related methodological issue pertains to the place of dogma in theological argumentation. Should we take the ecclesiastical decisions of the fourth and fifth centuries as our point of departure? Or should we begin with the New Testament instead? Or is this perhaps a false contrast, since according to the promise of John 16:13, the Spirit has been given to the church, with an implication that doctrinal developments may be accepted with thanksgiving as greater insight that has been given to the church? In other words, we have here the question of the role dogma ought to have in today's christological reflection. Do the councils form the

Logos and Spirit

hermeneutical framework within which the biblical data concerning Word and Spirit must be explained? Or could a rereading of Scripture produce a Spirit Christology that is not integrated into a Logos Christology? I would answer right away: no, it could not. According to a Reformed perspective, we cannot limit the role of dogmatics to a rational reflection on Chalcedon. The Bible must play a much more radical role.

A fine example of a sophisticated way of dealing with this methodological problem is offered by David Coffey. He gives an interesting attempt to say something about the relation between the immanent and the economic Trinity (i.e., between the Trinity eternally "in itself" and the Trinity as known historically in creation and redemption), while acknowledging the diversity of the witnesses in the New Testament Scriptures. Coffey incorporates a couple of methodological steps from Bernard Lonergan for his own Christology. First, we must work with biblical data, which is the primary material for later Trinitarian conceptualization. Starting with these data, an implicit concept of the Trinity arises.[4] In the New Testament, however, we see the Trinity only on a functional (or economic) level; the ontological (or immanent) framework is not yet fully elaborated. On the basis of the biblical data, then, a concept of the immanent Trinity was developed in the debates of the third and fourth centuries. The immanent Trinity is a theological category that aims to explain the way salvation history is anchored in God's own being. The next step in this process is that the concept of the immanent

4. David Coffey, *Deus Trinitas: The Doctrine of the Triune God* (New York: Oxford University Press, 1999), 15.

Trinity serves as the framework within which the biblical story and data are read and interpreted. This rereading leads to the concept of the economic Trinity. We thus can see that the concept of the immanent Trinity, itself a product of theological reflection, produces new theological knowledge.[5]

On the basis of biblical data, Coffey distinguishes between two models of the Trinity: a mission model and a return model.[6] Both models can be found in the Bible. The mission model can be identified with what P. Schoonenberg has labeled the ascending Christology of the Synoptic Gospels. Jesus, as the Spirit-anointed One, is sent by God and lives his life in obedience; in living this life, Jesus partakes in our life. The return model takes its vantage point from the immanent Trinity. The eternal Son becomes human, and his life is a return to the Father. It is established on the model of Philippians 2:5-11 or on the model of the Gospel of John.

The Role of Biblical Scholarship

Developments in biblical scholarship in the last few decades have given a new impulse to the question concerning Spirit Christology. New Testament scholarship has seen a growing confidence in the historicity of the gospel records. We can think in this context of the work of Larry Hurtado, Richard Bauckham, and Richard Hays,[7] among others. In his latest

---

5. Coffey, *Deus Trinitas*, 16-19.
6. Coffey, *Deus Trinitas*, 47-53.
7. Larry W. Hurtado, *Lord Jesus Christ: Devotion to Jesus in Earliest Christianity* (Grand Rapids: Eerdmans, 2003); Richard Bauckham, *Jesus and the Eyewitnesses: The Gospels as Eyewitness Testimony* (Grand Rapids:

book Michael Welker therefore refers to different levels of multicontextuality in what he calls "the Fourth Quest":[8] the impact of Jesus is not founded on the Easter reports alone; rather, in the mirror represented by the different gospel reports on the earthly Jesus, we see a number of different facets emerge of who he was. These reports have become particularly important for the pneumatological shift in theology in general and in particular for exploring the possibilities offered by a Spirit Christology. By itself, this shift does not mean that things are in any way simplified for systematic theology. From a theological point of view, it would actually be less complex to take one's starting point in Chalcedon, for example, and to continue reflecting on its logic. Such an approach, however, leaves the Bible largely on the sidelines, a position that I consider indefensible.

Progress in systematic theology and in pneumatology requires close dialogue with biblical scholarship. This dialogue is a *conditio sine qua non* for a theology that claims to have Reformed (biblical) roots. The hermeneutical task of theology for the church consists in an ongoing dialectical movement between reading and interpreting the Scriptures on the one hand and systematic reflection on the other. The priority, however, in that ongoing conversation must be the reading of God's Word and our interaction with God through that same Word. The role of biblical scholarship in that process is that of a guardian or keeper of a collective memory. It reminds the church of its former debates, decisions, and the various

---

Eerdmans, 2006); Beverly Roberts Gaventa and Richard B. Hays, eds., *Seeking the Identity of Jesus: A Pilgrimage* (Grand Rapids: Eerdmans, 2008).

8. Michael Welker, *God the Revealed: Christology* (Grand Rapids: Eerdmans, 2013), 87-94.

paths that have been trodden.[9] These paths and decisions are not just behind us; it is a worthwhile undertaking to test them every once in a while, since they show the church something of its past tensions and decisions that are still relevant. They also demonstrate to us the *nature* of our knowledge, namely, that this knowledge has come down to us along a human, historical path. It pleased God to meet us in these historical and literary processes. The texts in the Bible are the primary material for theology to work with, offering us insight into the process of experience, transmission, selection, reinterpretation, and appropriation. Along this process, biblical scholarship reminds us of the various ways in which Jesus Christ has been experienced and interpreted in the Bible.

Awareness of this differentiation within Scripture makes it impossible to read it in the light of later dogmatic development alone. Applied to the relationship of the role of the Pneuma to the role of the Logos, it means that multiple trajectories can be distinguished within the New Testament that sometimes cross and influence each other, although they always retain their own perspective. Systematically, it is important to be aware that it was possible to confess Jesus as Lord without appealing, for example, to a preexistent Logos. In this context, we can distinguish between an "ascending Christology" and a "descending Christology" (or to use the terminology of David Coffey, a "return-model Christology"). One should not identify an ascending Christology with a "low" Christology. The ascending Christology of Luke, for example, is a "high" Christology, in which Jesus Christ

---

9. See C. van der Kooi, "Kirche als Lesegemeinschaft: Schrifthermeneutik und Kanon," *VF* 51 (2006): 63-72.

Logos and Spirit

is confessed as Lord, as one who is worthy to be worshiped (Luke 24:52).[10]

An important element in the criticism of a Logos Christology was the claim that this classic doctrine rendered it impossible to take certain New Testament texts at face value; that is, that such a Christology is docetic. The New Testament reports that Jesus grew and became strong, was filled with wisdom (Luke 2:40), learned sonship by obedience (Heb. 5:8), and in the garden of Gethsemane prayed that the cup might be removed from him (Luke 22:42; Matt. 26:39; Mark 14:36), all of which can hardly be accounted for within a Logos Christology, if at all. Accordingly, it has been proposed that such details must be read in reference to his human nature, an approach that creates a tension with respect to the one person Jesus. In short, the humanity of the one person Jesus—that is, his historicity—is not accounted for as it should be within a Christology that is fully determined by the Logos doctrine. From a historical and systematic point of view, it is worth remembering that, before the fourth century, the concepts of Spirit and Word were used ambiguously and interchangeably.[11]

In Judaic Christianity, telling examples can be found of the opinion that, at Jesus's baptism, the Spirit came down on Jesus and consecrated him as Messiah and Son.[12] Also, with the Apostolic Fathers, the terms *logos* and *pneuma* are intermingled. In the Epistle of Barnabas, we find the expres-

---

10. Hurtado, *Lord Jesus Christ*, 340-46, esp. 345.

11. See G. C. van de Kamp, *Pneuma-christologie, een oud antwoord op een actuele vraag?* (Amsterdam: Rodopi, 1983).

12. A. Adam, *Lehrbuch der Dogmengeschichte*, vol. 1 (Gütersloh: Mohn, 1970), 156-58.

sion "vessel of the [Holy] Spirit" for the body of Jesus.[13] Thus an analogy exists between Christ and his followers because Christians belong to Christ because of their baptism. Second Clement states that, before the incarnation, Christ was *pneuma*, or Spirit.[14] Ignatius of Antioch states that Jesus is flesh and Spirit; according to his flesh, he belongs to us, and according to the Spirit, he belongs to God. There is a very significant assertion in the Shepherd of Hermas: "The Holy Spirit which pre-exists, which created all creation, did God make to dwell in the flesh which he willed. Therefore this flesh, in which the Holy Spirit dwelled, served the Spirit well, walking in holiness and purity, and did not in any way defile the spirit."[15] The older liberal theology used such data as an argument to reject a "high" Logos Christology in favor of a "low" Spirit Christology. But this argument now fails because we know that devotion to Jesus already existed in the earliest forms of Christianity and cannot be dismissed as a later addition. It is possible to put one's faith and trust in Jesus as Savior and Good Shepherd while also believing he is Spirit and Son.

Experience

In the first section of this chapter, we considered several reasons for reflecting further on the possibility of a Spirit Christology. One reason was a rereading of Scripture; a second reason addressed the risk of a docetic view of Jesus inherent

13. Barnabas 7.3.
14. 2 Clement 9.5.
15. Hermas, Similitudes 5.6.5 (59.5).

Logos and Spirit

to the Logos Christology model. A third and highly interesting reason is current experience. At certain moments experience can play a role as a source for renewed reflection. It can be a context of discovery, if not one of justification. The first examples that come to mind are those that have been felt all along in Pentecostal circles and in the charismatic renewal. Experiences of God's presence or experiences of recovery, healing, prophecy, patience, and empowerment in situations of brokenness all caused the conviction to grow in faith communities that the gospel reports were to be read with new glasses.[16] We might also mention the many liberation theologies that are rooted in social practices and experiences. Such experiences of liberation and shalom are like keys by which the Scriptures can be read anew. They lead to interesting projects in which churches of the Northern and Southern Hemispheres learn to communicate with each other in intercultural Bible-reading projects. The context of the one opens the eyes of the other to the Scriptures.

Liberation theology has repeatedly pointed to situations in which people in a certain circumstance of suffering or oppression began once more to experience the liberating power

---

16. "The exceptional growth and development of the Charismatic Renewal within all the Christian denominations throughout the world has not only revitalized interest in the Holy Spirit, but also, through the experience of Baptism in the Spirit, fostered a renewed and discernible awareness of the Christian's particular relationships with the individual persons of the Trinity. Baptism in the Spirit has confirmed, in an experiential manner, the love of the Father and the Lordship of Jesus the Son. Thus the Charismatic Renewal has both cultivated and provided factual evidence for the spiritual and practical relevance of the Trinity within the Christian's life." T. Weinandy, *The Father's Spirit of Sonship: Reconceiving the Trinity* (Edinburgh: T&T Clark, 1995), 4. See also ix and 107.

of the gospel. From a methodological perspective, this dynamic is important. At such moments, theological reflection does not run from the Bible to today; rather, today's experiences unlock certain parts of the Scriptures for its readers. It makes us aware that the same Spirit who was at work in Jesus Christ is also active today. Theologically and hermeneutically, the focus shifts from a biblical deposit that has been given once and for all to a process of reception, reading, obedience, and following.[17] This is the background to the issue of discernment (or discretion) for learning to know God's will and way. It is striking that in those communities where, on the basis of communal practices, the members have recovered the meaning of Christ and discovered or rediscovered new elements in the narrative of Jesus, the infamous "ugly ditch" (events in the past serving as proofs for the truth of Christian faith today) of which Lessing spoke is simply absent. The revivals and Pentecostal renewals of the last centuries have called for renewed attention for the specific role of the Holy Spirit as a protagonist in the life of the church. This experience directs us to an important implication of a Spirit-Christology approach: the same Spirit who was upon Jesus will also manifest himself in the lives of Jesus's followers.

The suggestion that the Spirit is an agent who guides the church by a variety of experiences can be found in the Scriptures themselves. The means by which the Spirit of Christ leads are diverse, including by witness, proclamation, sacraments, dreams, visions, or a long, enduring experience. The Gospel of

17. G. Sauter, "'Schrifttreue' ist kein 'Schriftprinzip,'" in *Offenbarung und Geschichten*, ed. John Barton and Gerhard Sauter (Frankfurt: Peter Lang, 2000), 21-49.

Logos and Spirit

John gives a clear indication of the future disclosures of the work of Christ: "I still have many things to say to you, but you cannot bear them now. When the Spirit of truth comes, he will guide you into all the truth; for he will not speak on his own, but will speak whatever he hears, and he will declare to you the things that are to come. He will glorify me, because he will take what is mine and declare it to you" (John 16:12-14). A very clear example of guidance by the Spirit in a process of discernment appears in Acts 10 and 11. Peter, informed by a vision and the voice of the Spirit, is gradually persuaded that the regulations regarding clean and unclean are renewed and are fulfilled in Christ. "What God has made clean, you must not call profane" (Acts 10:15). The Spirit pushes the young Jewish Christian community beyond a border that it would never have crossed on its own initiative.[18] This incident clarifies the question of the agency of the Holy Spirit in the present, or the discernment nowadays of the Spirit. The Spirit glorifies Jesus Christ in the present time; that is, the Spirit will fulfill and complete what has already become real in Jesus Christ. The meaning and impact of his life and work will be manifest in a multitude of new situations and contexts. When our time, according to the New Testament, is called eschatological time, it means that God has taken possession of our time and space in order to become manifest and address us.[19] How can we get to know the voice and will of God from among all the other voices?[20] In chapter 6 I will consider this question

18. H. Wuhrer, *Zum Stellenwert vom "Reden Gottes" im NT am Beispiel der Apostelgeschichte* (Amsterdam: VU Press, 2013).

19. G. Sauter, *In der Freiheit des Geistes* (Göttingen: Vandenhoeck & Ruprecht, 1987), 106.

20. Gaventa and Hays, "Seeking the Identity of Jesus," in *Seeking the Identity of Jesus: A Pilgrimage*, 1-24, esp. 17-22. See also P. G. R. de Villiers,

more explicitly, but for now a few remarks on the subject must be made because they are directly related to the search for the identity of Jesus and the anointing with the Holy Spirit.

The conviction that Christ also speaks today in the power of the Spirit, rather than being shut up in the past, is not new to Reformed theology but in recent theological reflection has found greater structural recognition and been given a greater sense of urgency. The Spirit does not work apart from one's own, context-specific experiences and outside of the community in which one lives and of which one is a part—but he indeed uses them. This insight is supported by hermeneutics and pneumatology.

Spirit Christology and Logos Christology: Three Models

How, then, do Spirit Christology and Logos Christology relate to each other? I distinguish three models, each of which can be found in the contemporary debate. I have labeled them substitute, alternative, and complementary, distinctions that have a merely heuristic function.

Substitute Model

The first option is taken by those theologians who want to replace the Logos Christology with a Spirit Christology. They consider Spirit Christology to be the better option, one that ought

---

ed., *The Spirit That Guides: Discernment in the Bible and Spirituality* (Bloemfontein: University of the Free State, 2013).

to replace, to substitute for, Logos Christology. These theologians are sometimes referred to as post-Trinitarian,[21] and they include a number of important nineteenth-century historical theologians, such as Adolf von Harnack, Reinhold Seeberg, and Friedrich Loofs, and more recently the theologians Paul Tillich, Geoffrey Lampe, Hendrikus Berkhof, James Dunn, and Richard Haight; from the Netherlands, I would include Gerrit van de Kamp and Gijs Dingemans (Berkhof and Haight will be further discussed in chapter 3). The decisive argument supporting this position includes the charge that a Logos Christianity in fact threatens the humanity of Jesus. According to the proponents of a Spirit Christology, the Logos Christology represents an impediment for people today because the meaning of the concepts "nature" and "person," which are basic to this position, has shifted, rendering them incomprehensible in the present context. From that perspective these terms do more harm than good. Seeberg and Harnack point out that, in the writings of the Apostolic Fathers, the uniqueness of Jesus was not interpreted in terms of the Logos alone but also in terms of the Spirit. The ecumenical creeds, it is therefore argued, have overshadowed and suppressed the possibility of expressing the significance of the person and work of Jesus Christ in terms of the Spirit. The doctrine of the hypostatic union of the divine and human natures in the person of the eternal Logos represents an overly static or "object-like" interpretation of the identity of Jesus. Accordingly, his human history begins to look all too much like the mechanical following of a predetermined script.[22]

21. Myk Habets, *The Anointed Son: A Trinitarian Spirit Christology* (Eugene, OR: Pickwick Publications, 2010).
22. G. Lampe, *God as Spirit* (Oxford: Oxford University Press, 1979); van de Kamp, *Pneuma-christologie*; P. Schoonenberg, *De Geest, het Woord*

The critique of Logos Christology by these theologians amounted to a radical criticism of the christological and Trinitarian doctrines as such[23] and was related to their presupposition that a "higher" Logos Christology was in fact a later development in the history of the church. In fact, the particularity of Jesus Christ as not only coming from God but as being divine was rejected. On the other side, the advantage of a pneumatological approach must also be praised. Jesus is seen foremost as a human being, one of us, who is in many ways different and higher in morality and awareness of God. Nevertheless, the ideal of the life of Jesus as exemplary, as someone who is called to follow his way of being human, should not be dismissed. In early Christianity, with its emphasis on discipleship, the kingdom of God, and living according to the Sermon on the Mount, Jesus was not only Redeemer but, as Redeemer, the one who also must be followed.

Given the influence of the role played in this development by the liberal camp, the term "Spirit Christology" was long associated with a radical critique of the church's doctrine; after all, the very divinity of Jesus was at stake![24] With Wilhelm

---

en de Zoon (Kampen: Kok, 1991); J. Hick, *The Metaphor of God Incarnate: Christology in a Pluralistic Age*, 2nd ed. (Louisville: Westminster John Knox, 2005); G. D. J. Dingemans, *Het menselijk gezicht van God: Jezus als de unieke drager van de Geest* (Kampen: Kok, 2003).

23. In distinction from Myk Habets, I prefer the term "substitute" instead of "post-Trinitarian." The prefix "post" suggests a temporal order that, in the light of the contemporary renaissance of Trinitarian thought, no longer seems appropriate.

24. The opinion that Logos Christology is an impediment for contemporary thought and culture was put forward much earlier by Friedrich Schleiermacher. His critique of the doctrine of the two natures because of the changed meaning of the concept of nature cannot be dismissed as an attempt to transform Jesus Christ into an ordinary human being or to

Logos and Spirit

Bousset, many came to view the confession of the divinity of Jesus as a later development in an originally Palestinian or Aramaic Christianity. If I am not mistaken, this association is no longer as readily made today as it once was. The plea for a reevaluation of the pneumatological dimension in Jesus's life and therefore the reappropriation of Christology as a Spirit Christology accordingly also comes from quarters that can hardly be characterized as liberal and that have no interest in discarding Chalcedon. This shift in the theological landscape owes a lot to the developments in biblical scholarship we already noted above. The positions have shifted considerably; the assumption that a high Christology was a "glorification" of the earthly Jesus has proved in fact to be no longer tenable.[25] This development has led to greater receptivity in more theologically orthodox contexts to reflections on Spirit Christology. As a result, it is now possible to relate one's own faith *in* Jesus more closely to the faith *of* Jesus.

Alternative Model

As a second possibility for relating Spirit and Logos Christologies, I identify a model for which the Dutch theologian Piet Schoonenberg was once the most important spokesperson. This model can be called alternative. In it, Spirit Christology

---

transpose Christology into anthropology. This negative interpretation of Schleiermacher by Karl Barth has had a lasting influence on the reception of Schleiermacher's Christology. But it misunderstands Schleiermacher's intention to build up Christology, which on its own terms must be labeled "high," in terms of Spirit. See chapter 4.

25. Note the aforementioned publications of Hurtado and Bauckham.

and Logos Christology relate to each other as alternatives; that is, they are two parallel but different avenues within the one canon for expressing what was so unique about Jesus Christ. Schoonenberg has insisted that they are each independently able to say everything that ought to be said in a Christology. I, however, have my doubts about this latter claim. Is it possible to express everything that belongs to a Christology in terms of the Spirit? In the next chapter, I will give my reasons for this doubt.[26] What I do consider possible is to understand the relation between Logos Christology and Spirit Christology in the sense of a mutual complementarity: two lines that mutually complete and interpret the other. That is the third option.

Complementary Model

The third option, which receives a lot of support today, holds that Spirit Christology is a substantial complement to the Logos tradition. It means that we take our starting point in the church's official pronouncements on Trinity and Christology from the fourth and fifth centuries and attempt to fill them with pneumatological elements. As one of its presuppositions, this option understands the church to have been correct when it decided to express the identity of Jesus using the phrase "true God" and "true man." The proponents of this model include such authors as Robert Jenson, Harold Hunter, and Myk Habets, as well as Roman Catholic theologians David Coffey, Ralph del Colle, Thomas Weinandy, and others.

---

26. Schoonenberg, *De Geest, het Woord en de Zoon*, 27.

Logos and Spirit

In support of this model we can also include the work of Pope Benedict XVI.

I note, first, that there is a clear difference between Protestant and Roman Catholic participants in this discussion. Most Catholic theologians hold that we cannot go back behind the church's doctrinal pronouncements; for them, the doctrinal determinations of the ecumenical synods are the point of departure for the church's liturgy, as well as for its teaching. Many Protestant theologians, in contrast, argue that these determinations do not in the first place owe their authority to the church but are authoritative because and insofar as they are supported by Scripture or can be defended in a contemporary intellectual context. This is not to deny that there are many Protestants—especially Presbyterians—who on a practical level also take their starting point from the decisions of the church. As such, they place themselves in the broader catholic and Trinitarian trajectory that a number of important Protestant confessional documents explicitly follow. The Belgic Confession, for example, states that it accepts the decisions of the early church. The Heidelberg Catechism clearly confesses the divinity of Father, Son, and Spirit, and no less clear is the statement made in this regard by the Westminster Confession. Also a modern reappropriation of Chalcedon, as apparent in the work of Karl Barth, can be located on this trajectory; as modernized as it may be, it in essence still comes down to being a reinterpretation of Chalcedon. Nonetheless, by establishing the biblical foundation (i.e., revelation itself) as the critical moment, as *norma normans* at center stage, one would be altogether warranted to subject the church in its doctrinal pronouncements to a critical examination. Such a process leaves Chalcedon and its Logos Christology not unchanged!

Second, I call this approach "complementary" because it reintroduces pneumatological elements in the biblical witness that were forgotten or suppressed, which serves to deepen and enrich Logos Christology. However, if the pneumatological dimension in Jesus's life receives so fundamental an emphasis as it does in the thought of David Coffey, for example, such that the Logos concept also comes to be radically colored by it, we might speak rather of mutual complementarity. In this model, Logos Christology and Spirit Christology are understood to be two approaches that, as distinct methods of christological reflection, interpret and need each other. The mutuality is essential.

In the next chapter I will argue in favor of a Spirit Christology in which the filial and the pneumatic elements affect each other. That is, Logos Christology is reinterpreted through attributing an essential role to the Spirit; Word and Spirit presuppose and interpret each other. The Son is the Son in the power of the Spirit. This understanding has far-reaching consequences. Among other things, it means that we cannot understand the term "Logos" in terms of an unchangeable divine principle from which we can determine a priori what that divinity includes. If the incarnation of the Logos in the Gospel of John refers to the man Jesus Christ, then we should learn from his life and person what Logos means. That is, we can no longer think of the Logos apart from who Jesus Christ was, from how he behaved, obeying the one whom he called Father. The Logos cannot be understood apart from Jesus Christ seeking his way, trying to discern his calling, and becoming, as Hebrews 12:2 says, "the pioneer and perfecter of our faith." In all this, Jesus as human being comes closer to us. But there is more to say here. When Pneuma and Logos presuppose and interpret each other, then the Logos and divinity can no longer be understood as unchangeable divine principles but as having the ability to assume what is human, weak, and restricted. Put briefly, this assumption confirms a feature that can be encountered on many occasions in God's story with Israel, namely, God's susceptibility to human weakness and limitation.

3 The Anointed Son
Toward a Sustainable Spirit-Christology

Some Proposals for a Spirit Christology

Does Spirit Christology not run the risk of removing the particularity of Jesus Christ when the Spirit is poured out on everyone? The critical counterquestion would be whether the Bible itself does not almost deny Christ's particularity when, for instance, Paul in Romans 8:29 writes that we are coheirs with Jesus Christ and when Paul uninhibitedly and interchangeably calls believers children. This claim is enormous. The same Spirit who rested on Jesus will take hold of human beings and the world and bring them to glory. All this is not yet present, and at the same time it is already emerging. But if so, what is the difference between Christ and those who are his? In a Spirit Christology, all such questions are relevant, and I seek to answer them in this chapter. In the first part, I briefly discuss the contributions of Roger Haight, Hendrikus Berkhof, Piet Schoonenberg, Patrick Lens, and David Coffey according to the three models that were initially introduced in the previous chapter. Subsequently, I develop my own constructive proposal.

Toward a Sustainable Spirit-Christology

Substitute Model: Roger Haight and Hendrikus Berkhof

I start with Roger Haight, who has defended a form of Christology that falls in the model of Spirit Christology as substituting for Logos Christology. God is Spirit, and all that God does must be understood in terms of Spirit. The same applies also to Jesus. "Jesus was a person in whom was recognized the presence, power, and action of God in such a measure, that Jesus was conceived as God's agent."[1] Haight regards it as a category mistake when one of the works of God in history is objectified or reified. The belief that Jesus Christ is the eternal Son of God is an example of such an objectification or reification. Behind this criticism stands a symbol theory. A symbol is, according to Haight, "that through which something other than itself is known. A symbol mediates awareness of something else."[2] The concept of awareness is crucial in this theology. The word "awareness" is "not at all used to be dismissive about the character of the kind of cognition that religion implies; it is not an attenuated form of cognition." It is in its own generic way cognitive. Religious language invites us to a

---

1. Roger Haight, *Jesus, Symbol of God* (Maryknoll, NY: Orbis, 1999), 166.
2. Haight, *Jesus, Symbol of God*, 8. See also Manuela Kalsky, *Christaphanien: Die Revision der Christologie aus der Sicht von Frauen in unterschiedlichen Kulturen* (Gütersloh: Gütersloher Verlagshaus, 2000), 325: "Christaphanien sollen die Erinnerung an den Begriff der Epiphanien wach halten, an die plötzlichen und erwarteten Momente, in denen das Heilige erscheinen/geschehen kann." But this view evidently leads to another position of Jesus: "Er ist ein Exponent in der Hoffnung auf und im Glauben and die verheissene messianische Zeit, ein Wegweiser Gottes, gebunden an einen bestimmten Ort, eine bestimmte Zeit und ein bestimmtes Geschlecht" (329).

participatory experience of something that is beyond human control but nevertheless exposes itself to the human mind.[3]

In his theology, Haight shows himself to be a student of Karl Rahner in that the thematically unconscious awareness of God's self-communication becomes categorical in historical experiences. In this general way, it can be said that Jesus is the symbol of God. Jesus is, in the Christian community, the one through whom salvation from God is mediated.[4] It is important to see that Rahner's concept of the difference between transcendental and categorical revelation is decisive in Haight's Christology. It provides him with the possibility of a sharp feeling for the endless qualitative distinction between eternity and time. He turns this tool of interpreting the biblical and creedal concepts into a weapon against the very one to whom he owes much: Karl Rahner. Rahner has interpreted divine revelation, or, in his own words, God's self-communication, as a mystery that is structurally located within the human horizon; as transcendent being, the human being already has awareness of a border and an infinity that offers itself graciously.[5] The hypostatic union is interpreted as the final acceptance of God's self-communication. When Rahner declares that God was decisively present in Jesus Christ as Logos, Haight asks the question, For what reason is this hypostatic union possible only once? Why should Christ be unique? "There is no hard reason why God could not approach humanity in a variety of ways and in more than one

---

3. Haight, *Jesus, Symbol of God*, 9, 11.
4. Haight, *Jesus, Symbol of God*, 426.
5. Karl Rahner, *Grundkurs des Glaubens: Einführung in den Begriff des Christentums* (Freiburg: Herder, 1976), 67–76.

medium."⁶ The uniqueness of the revelation in Jesus Christ is hereby questioned. It seems clear that the hermeneutical-philosophical interpretation of the symbolic nature of all religious language prevents Haight from personifying the concept of Word. When Jesus is called Word, it is a metaphoric way of expression. Every manner of personification is overridden by the following claim he makes: "The hypostatization and reification of Logos is a fundamental distortion of religious understanding and predication."⁷ As a consequence, the divinity of Jesus Christ can mean only that people have encountered grace from God in Jesus. According to Haight, however, it should not mean that the person of Jesus is somehow unique, for grace can be found in many places. However, exactly that element of the identity of Jesus was pivotal in the decisions of the church in the fourth century.

A second example of a full-blown Spirit Christology that is meant as a substitute for a Logos Christology is offered by Hendrikus Berkhof, not only in his *Christian Faith* but already in his Warfield Lectures. Just like Schoonenberg, he is firmly convinced that the unity of Christ and his true humanity must be maintained, and for that reason he distances himself from Chalcedon. For the model of the two natures he substitutes his concept of the covenant. Jesus was sent to fulfil the covenant of God with Israel. Because the sons of Israel failed, Jesus had to bring this covenant to its completion in his life. Therefore, this son of Israel is named the Son. The concept of Son should therefore be understood as a covenantal concept. Jesus is not the eternal Logos; instead, he is the covenantal

6. Haight, *Jesus, Symbol of God*, 433.
7. Haight, *Jesus, Symbol of God*, 441.

partner who is brought into being by a particular creative act of God, which Berkhof identifies as an act of God's Spirit. Jesus is filled with the Holy Spirit in an abundant and complete way. His subjectivity—his "I"—is completely absorbed by the Holy Spirit. This abundant presence of the Holy Spirit in Jesus makes it possible that he can be the faithful covenantal partner who does not fail. Because of this victory over sin and estrangement from God, Jesus is exalted and given rule over the world.

With this substitute model of Spirit Christology, it is clear that Berkhof is no longer able to support the doctrine of the Trinity. This doctrine is a description of the fulfilled covenant. The covenant between God and human beings is fulfilled in Christ and is opened by the Holy Spirit to include Christ's fellow human beings. The Holy Spirit, however, is not a separate person from Jesus Christ. By appealing to 2 Corinthians 3:17a, Berkhof identifies the Holy Spirit with the exalted Christ acting in history. Just like Schoonenberg, Berkhof presents a highly dynamic view of God. As he said as early as 1964: "These names [Spirit-Son-Father] in their togetherness point to a movement of the one God, not a static community of three persons. They are the description of an ongoing movement of condescendence, in which God reaches out deeper and deeper toward man in his sin and distress, until in the end he can touch the heart of the individual by his regenerating power in the Spirit of Christ. Then the Spirit leads to Christ, and in Christ man finds God."[8] The Trinitarian language in this quotation is a function of the saving movement of God. Not without reason,

8. Berkhof, *Doctrine of the Holy Spirit*, 116.

Toward a Sustainable Spirit-Christology

Berkhof also points to the theology of fourth-century theologian Marcellus of Ancyra as a brave attempt to historicize the Trinitarian categories.[9] In distinction from Marcellus, Berkhof does not expect a renewal of Trinitarian thought from a discovery of the biblical content of the term "Logos"; rather, it will come from discovering the term "Spirit."

Alternative Model: Piet Schoonenberg

In the foregoing chapter, Piet Schoonenberg (1911-99) was mentioned as a theologian who has offered an interesting and deep proposal that falls within the alternative model. More than anyone else, he reflects in his work the historical and cultural background of the modern search for a Spirit Christology, namely, the question of the ontological status of the humanity of Jesus Christ, which was particularly raised in the nineteenth century.[10] What does it mean to confess the humanity of Christ? In the history of the Renaissance and Enlightenment, increased attention was given to the human being as subject. This emphasis also raises questions when it comes to Jesus Christ as a fully human subject. If Christ is fully human, does this not include human self-consciousness and a kind of autonomy as well? When Jesus prays to the Fa-

---

9. See J. Pelikan, *The Emergence of the Catholic Tradition (100-600)*, vol. 1 of *The Christian Tradition: A History of the Development of Doctrine* (Chicago: University of Chicago Press, 1971), 207-8.

10. Schoonenberg, *De Geest, het Woord en de Zoon*; Patrick Lens, "Schoonenberg en de uniciteit van Christus," in *Verleden openen naar heden en toekomst: Meedenken met de christologie van Piet Schoonenberg*, ed. T. Merrigan and K. Struys (Averbode: Altiora, 2001), 81-98.

ther, should we suppose two divine subjects in converse? Is it possible to understand the incarnation of the Son in terms of the intrinsic creational capacities within nature itself? From a modern perspective the Logos in Logos Christology seems to be an intrusive element that remains strange and effects a dichotomy in the person of Christ. Schoonenberg, however, has consistently emphasized that he does not want to get rid of the Logos Christology. In his view, both Logos Christology and Spirit Christology offer an avenue to articulate the particularity of the work and person of Jesus Christ. His proposal thus falls within the alternative model.

In developing his Christology, he has tried to give a proper answer to the problem of traditional Logos Christology, namely, the risk that the vocabulary of Logos Christology in fact favors a docetic understanding of Jesus Christ.

In his earlier work, Schoonenberg became famous, if not notorious, for his use of the doctrine of the *enhypostatic union*. According to orthodox doctrine, the Logos is the supporting and decisive denominator in Jesus Christ for uniting the divine and human natures hypostatically (i.e., as a personal reality). The human nature is not thought of as a human being as such, which means, according to Schoonenberg, that the human nature must be thought of as anhypostatic. It is the eternal Logos who dwells hypostatically in and bears the human nature.

It is clear that such a solution originally was meant to avoid the conclusion of a doubleness in Jesus. But at the same time, this approach casts a shadow on understanding Jesus as fully human. The person of the Son is there (in the human nature of Christ) from eternity, and the incarnation does not bring any change to the person of the eternal Son.

Toward a Sustainable Spirit-Christology

Schoonenberg tries to solve the problem by starting with the human nature as the point of departure, not with the eternal Logos. When Jesus is fully human, we then have to say that the Word, or eternal Logos, cannot be fully person in the modern way of understanding because "person" means in modernity a center of freedom and self-consciousness. If we think of the Logos in this way, as person, we come to the idea of a community of three gods. Schoonenberg argued that the Logos as person can stand over against the Father only in the human consciousness of Jesus.[11] For that reason Schoonenberg sought a solution by what he called an "inverted enhypostasis." He no longer wanted to see the eternal Logos as the central personalizing element in Jesus Christ but the other way around: his humanity as the personalizing element. Schoonenberg therefore once spoke in his work of the anhypostatic nature of the divine Logos in Christ; rather, the divine Logos is enhypostatic in the human nature of Jesus.[12] By entering a process of becoming, of change under the human condition, the figure of the Logos becomes personalized. The humanity of Christ is thus the supporting and most significant factor that effects an ongoing process of becoming a person for the Logos. In this process, the Spirit as the power of God, which surfaces in the Old Testament as Wisdom or the Spirit, is the decisive factor in the life and acts of Jesus. Schoonenberg regards the concept of Wisdom as the biblical link between the two movements of Spirit and Word.

11. Patrick Lens, "God heeft zich aan onze menselijkheid gewaagd," *Comm* 21 (1996): 375.
12. Piet Schoonenberg, *The Christ: A Study of the God-Man Relationship in the Whole of Creation and in Jesus Christ* (New York: Herder & Herder, 1972), 87.

What to say of this undeniably creative attempt to safeguard the full humanity of Christ? We need to raise the question as to what exactly the Logos or Wisdom is in this concept. Is it a *sphere of divinity* that becomes personalized only in the human self-consciousness of Jesus?

As noted, in later publications Schoonenberg declared that his proposals were not meant to eliminate Logos Christology but were a plea for a *complementary* approach by which the one-sidedness of the Logos Christology could be avoided. Logos Christology and Spirit Christology are two avenues in the biblical material that can mutually interpret each other without collapsing their distinction.

It should be clear that this concept also has a deep significance for the doctrine of God. God is no longer understood as a being without change. In sending Jesus and in sending his Spirit, God becomes a participant in history. And it can even be said that God in this history becomes enriched. Schoonenberg's sympathy for Marcellus of Ancyra is clear. Just like Marcellus, Schoonenberg wants to emphasize the unity of God; the distinctions of Son and Spirit are not eternal in the Godhead, but only temporary and "economic." The Logos is not distinct from God; rather, it is God in action. I will come back to this theory later. The least one can say is that this is a stirring solution to an old problem: how to avoid a kind of tritheism and how to take the humanity of Jesus Christ with full seriousness. The deepest question in all this discussion is whether human reality can be the bearer of divinity.

What do these ideas mean for the question of the relation between Logos Christology and Spirit Christology? Schoonenberg's conclusion is that the New Testament knows a Spirit Christology, by which what identifies Jesus as the Son is contributed by the Spirit. The complete bestowal with God's pneuma is determinative for the Sonship of Christ. I doubt, however, whether the relation can be stated that causally. For sure, it is true that the Spirit of God is a fundamental factor during the whole of Jesus's life and in his Sonship. Schoonenberg's claim, however, goes one step further—namely, that the Spirit *makes* Jesus the Son.

Complementary Model: David Coffey

A recent and interesting example of a Spirit Christology that I mention briefly is presented by David Coffey. In distinction from the proposals of Haight, Berkhof, and Schoonenberg, Coffey's proposal remains within traditional boundaries of the Trinitarian concept of a hypostatic union with the eternal Son. Nevertheless, the bestowal of the Holy Spirit on Jesus plays a dominant role in his Christology.[13] The sanctifying grace of the Holy Spirit (*gratia habitualis*) is not something that follows the grace of union (*gratia unionis*) but is the foundation of the latter. The focus on the human life of Jesus and his Abba experience means a shift of interest: the interpretation of the identity of Jesus should not focus exclusively on the Paschal mystery, as in the theologies of Jürgen Moltmann and Eberhard Jüngel, but on the presence and activity of the Holy Spirit in the life of Jesus, from its beginning to its end. The Gospels of Matthew and Luke give ample testimony to the bestowal of the Spirit as the founding event of the life of

13. David Coffey, "The Theandric Nature of Christ," *TS* 60 (1999): 405–31.

Jesus; the work of the Spirit brings Jesus into existence (Matt. 1:18–25; Luke 1:26–38). The action and presence of the Spirit are therefore the dynamic factors that drive Jesus throughout his life:

> The Spirit is the love of the Father for Jesus, poured out on him in a radical and unique way and experienced as such on the part of Jesus. The Spirit, through the answering love it evoked from him, enabled him to live his whole life in dedicated obedience to the Father's will. All this comes to expression in Jesus' consciousness in the manner of his address of God in prayer, Abba, my Father. Where previously the Spirit has been seen only as God's power, as in the creation, and as his inspiration, as in the prophets . . . now in the case of Jesus it is revealed as his love.[14]

The difference from Schoonenberg is that Coffey clarifies the relationship of the Holy Spirit to the Father and the Son by the help of what he calls the return model, or the concept of the immanent Trinity. The bond of love with the Father that is realized and appropriated in the life of Jesus has its foundation in the inner life of God, in which the Holy Spirit is the objectification of the mutual love between Father and Son. By the special action of the Holy Spirit, Jesus has, in a human way, the same utter openness to, dependence on, and love for the Father that the Son has in the Trinity. Thus Coffey accepts and interprets what the church has validated on the level of teaching, namely, the formulations of the Holy Spirit in the

---

14. Coffey, *Deus Trinitas*, 37.

First Council of Constantinople and the dogmatization of the *filioque* in the Western church. He integrates what he calls a biblical doctrine of the Trinity within the broader context of the immanent Trinity, which he stipulates as the ontological condition of the functional divinity in the Scriptures.

I conclude these observations on Coffey by saying that his concept is a differentiated and thoughtful concept that integrates a dominant role for the Spirit within the framework of Trinitarian theology. For that reason it is one of the best proposals that I know. At the same time, the sharp distinction between functional and ontological is, in my opinion, problematic.

The Identity of Jesus

Having briefly discussed the proposals of Haight, Berkhof, Schoonenberg, and Coffey, I turn to answer the question at hand: How should we state the identity of Jesus? What is the proper role of Spirit and Word? The point of departure for theological reflection should be, first of all, the way Jesus is pictured in the New Testament. This is the focus, and if we can say something about Jesus's identity in relation to God's being, then it must be learned here. The variety of stories and images found in the New Testament can be summarized in three short statements:

1. Jesus has identified himself in his acts and prayer life with the God of Israel and the fulfillment of the promises for Israel.
2. The God of Israel has identified himself with Jesus in the

resurrection and exaltation, thereby confirming Jesus as his unique Son.
3. The identification wrought by the resurrection of Jesus is the final confirmation of the way Jesus is described in the Gospels: Jesus is the envoy of God, anointed with the eschatological Spirit, and completely directed to God as his Father.

By taking these three statements as a short summary, it is clear that, not only the paschal mystery should be a point of departure for Christology (which is faithful to the creeds without excluding Scripture), but the vantage point should be his whole life and work for the kingdom of God in light of the crucifixion and resurrection. The Bible points primarily and most specifically to the life of this one human being, Jesus of Nazareth, who identified himself in word and deed with the fulfillment of the promises for Israel and thereby for the world.

This salvation-historical perspective should remind us that the Gospels do not have two natures as a reference point but rather this one person as part of the long history of God and Israel. Although the dual-perspective model of a divine and human nature in one person is fully understandable, it carries an obvious disadvantage. The problem with such a definition is the suggestion that the mystery is the being together of two natures, divine and human.[15] The soteriological and divine element in the story of Jesus is, however, that God in this one human being assumes the whole project that he

---

15. Cornelis van der Kooi and Gijsbert van den Brink, *Christian Dogmatics: An Introduction* (Grand Rapids: Eerdmans, 2017), 400–402.

Toward a Sustainable Spirit-Christology

started with creation and the human condition as such. He fully engages in the history of Israel, in the still-open question of whether the covenant would be fulfilled. In the life and fate of Jesus Christ, God shows that God is able to come near in a situation where estrangement and guilt turn out to be dominant. According to the text of the Old Testament, God sometimes gets hurt, feels pain, would like to start over, and has to make up his mind. He is susceptible to what Israel does and how it behaves. We must start in our thinking with God's salvation history with Israel when we want to talk about God's divinity.

The reality of God's engagement in Jesus is made manifest in the Gospels by relational and dynamic language and images. Jesus as a person exists in full openness and obedience to God in God's reign over world and creation. Jesus allows himself to be fully determined by God. In his dedication to God, Jesus's existence is structurally "eccentric," that is, directed to God as his Father. Obviously, Jesus experienced God as an attachment figure,[16] calling him Abba and perceiving his own relation to God as a filial one. Put otherwise, his identity as Son consists in his being completely and freely determined by and responsive to God as his Father. In his being directed to God and his kingdom, he can also be perceived as the substantialization of the principle of gift and reception in God. This eccentricity is manifested, among other ways, in the Abba experience, which is a significant element in the prayer life of Jesus as found in the New Testament. The fact that this Aramaic *Fremdwort* appears in the New Testament

---

16. Bas van Os, *Psychological Analyses and the Historical Jesus: New Ways to Explore Christian Origins* (London: T&T Clark, 2011), 112.

is a sign that this filial experience in the life of Jesus is essential. For example, the filial dimension in the life of Jesus is also clear in Matthew 11:27: "All things have been handed over to me by my Father; and . . . no one knows the Father except the Son and anyone to whom the Son chooses to reveal him." The background of this image is likely the situation of a carpenter's workplace where a son learns the craft from his father. Also, the Gospel of John articulates this eccentricity explicitly: "For I have come down from heaven, not to do my own will, but the will of him who sent me" (John 6:38); and "I do nothing on my own, but I speak these things as the Father instructed me. And the one who sent me is with me; he has not left me alone, for I always do what is pleasing to him" (John 8:28-29).

This filial dimension is intertwined with the dynamic, creative, and transformative work of the Spirit in the life of Jesus. The Spirit as creative and formative power was, according to the Gospels of Matthew and Luke, present in the life of Jesus from the beginning in his conception. The Spirit, already at work in creation, is also determinative for the second Adam. There is continuity with discontinuity. He is born from Mary and so fully participates in human existence. And there is discontinuity: he is a new initiative of God in the story of this world. The presence of the eschatological Spirit in his life becomes manifest in that he brings justice and shalom, which come with the messianic rule. The sick are healed, lame people walk, the deaf can hear, and the poor are restored to justice. Because of the anointing with the Spirit of the eschaton, the darkness has to yield, and devilish powers are expelled (Mark 3:7-12). The Gospels characterize Jesus as self-conscious of being a charismatic healer and bearer of the eschatological Spirit.[17] In doing so, he is the Son, the Messiah. By his performance the firstfruits of this reign are tasted, the charisms, or gifts of grace. In the book of Acts, this ministry receives the short explanation "for God was with him" (10:38).

The challenge for contemporary systematic reflection is how the language of Sonship is related to the language of the Spirit and how these metaphors must be interpreted ontologically. Do they express ontological status? Is Sonship a result of being anointed with the Spirit or being bearer of the Spirit? Or the other way around: Is Jesus's being bearer of the Spirit already implied in his Sonship? The biblical material itself, courage to follow the evidence in the text, and the teaching of the church should give direction to our discourse and thoughts.

We saw that Word and Spirit, Sonship and being baptized by the Spirit, are two lines both present in the accounts, without necessarily being reduced to each other. There is good reason once again to remember the image of the two hands of God. This is metaphoric language, but it would be incorrect to regard such language as improper. On the contrary, metaphoric language specifies reality and carries ontological implications. The same criticism must be made in case a contradiction is suggested between functional and ontological. Such a suggestion testifies to a naive theological realism.[18] These ontological implications also apply for the concepts of Word and

---

17. J. Dunn, *Jesus and the Spirit: A Study of the Religious and Charismatic Experience of Jesus and the First Christians as Reflected in the New Testament* (London: SCM, 1975), 52-53.

18. See Welker, *God the Revealed*, 274-75, who refers among others to Janet Soskice, *The Kindness of God: Metaphor, Gender, and Religious Language* (Oxford: Oxford University Press, 2007), 7-9 and 157-58.

Spirit as used in the New Testament. In line with Schoonenberg, Word and Spirit can be qualified as self-movements of God toward creation and history. These processions of Word and Spirit are not sheer appropriations, not mere distinctions of the human mind, but are supported by the self-movement of God toward the world.[19] They have their source in the life of God. The question is, however, what this self-movement actually is. What is the Logos or the biblical background of it? Is wisdom a *sphere* in which Jesus is absorbed? In that case the Logos would be a sort of Christ-*principle*, and incarnation would be repeatable. This is exactly the opinion in many esoteric faith communities, such as anthroposophy. Or was Jesus Christ more than that? Is the Logos God in person who has entered our world and assumed our humanity? That is exactly the connotation for the christological concept of incarnation. The debate is decided through the question of whether there is an ontological ground in God's being for the Son as substantiation of God's own receptivity and what that ontological ground is. In other words, the question is whether one accepts an immanent Trinity.

I discuss briefly here the well-known distinction between functional and ontological. This distinction emerges from the observation that the concept of Sonship in the New Testament does not yet have the conceptual meaning that it assumed in later times. The same may be said even more truly regarding the Spirit: only rather later was the Spirit's divine status confessed in the Creed, and even then not directly. This all is not to deny that good reasons for such a settlement can be found in the Bible itself. We already mentioned the increasing

---

19. See Lens, "Schoonenberg en de uniciteit van Christus," 93.

Toward a Sustainable Spirit-Christology

personalization of the Spirit in Acts, with Paul, and in the Paraclete passage. This is even truer for the metaphor "son," historically a fluid concept that is transformed through its important role in Jesus's own experience of God. That is, the way Jesus himself relates to God has been decisive for the specification of the concept of Son. The language of Sonship therefore conversely serves to tell something of Jesus's own experience of God. The thing requiring interpretation (the *interpretandum*), namely, Jesus and his story, has a bearing on the interpretive construct (the *interpretamentum*), namely, Sonship. It is telling that the Bible gives remarkable information about Jesus's own filial experience: (1) the words spoken at his baptism by John the Baptist, (2) the way Jesus addressed God as Abba in his prayer life, and (3) the intimate image in Matthew 11:27 of the Son receiving all things from his Father. These data suggest a dyadic relationship between Jesus and God and point to a relation of origin that the NT attributes to no one else.[20] Paul can therefore predicate Jesus as God's *own* Son (Rom. 8:3, 32), the firstborn, or only, son. The rest of humanity possesses, in light of this one, the status of adopted children; they have received the Spirit of sonship. The connotation of unicity that surfaces is also manifest in the Johannine concept of Logos, when he applies the concept to the concrete, acting person of Jesus. As already said, the concept of Logos in John is historically related to the wisdom tradition and means, by and large, the ultimate coherence or sense of all things. By application to Jesus this concept is

---

20. Reinhard Feldmeier and Herrmann Spieckermann, *Der Gott der Lebendigen: Eine biblische Gotteslehre* (Tübingen: Mohr Siebeck, 2011), 66-92.

transposed. John 1:1 must be read from the perspective of the "I am" sayings in the following chapters, which all refer to the concrete Jesus (John 6:35; 8:58). Once again, the *interpretandum* has an effect for the *interpretamentum*, the concept of Logos.[21] This reversal of interpretation plays an important role within the preexistence sayings of the Gospel of John. It tells us that Jesus was already active from the beginning. He is original to God. And being original to God, he is the goal of God.

Unus de Trinitate

In this connection, I discuss the Belgian theologian Patrick Lens and his critique of the theology of Schoonenberg. Central to Lens's comments stands the question of how we can affirm the uniqueness of God that is attributed in the New Testament to Jesus Christ. Apart from his appreciation of Schoonenberg's theology, Lens advances the criticism that, for Schoonenberg, God's personal turning toward us is jeopardized. The language of inhabitation, although important, falls short when it comes to the ground of being in Jesus Christ.[22] In Schoonenberg's solution, the Word becomes hypostatic only in the life of Jesus.[23] Schoonenberg could therefore speak of the anhypostatic divine nature. On modern anthropological grounds this usage is understandable, but this strategy seems to restrict the involvement of God to the

21. Schoonenberg, *De Geest, het Woord en de Zoon*, 61-63, and P. Lens, "Op Hem bleef de Geest rusten," *Comm* 30 (2005): 23.
22. Lens, "Op Hem bleef de Geest rusten," 25.
23. Schoonenberg, *Het Woord, de Geest en de Zoon*, 93.

creaturely sphere; the divine principle is taken up by a human being and thus personified by the humanity of Jesus. In that case, "the human being Jesus is left as a non-divine subject in relation to the Father, without himself being the personal revelation of God in the categories of creation."[24] Incarnation would in principle be repeatable, because any human being could take up the divine principle. At issue is the question whether God himself enters history, or put otherwise, the question of whether Jesus Christ as person has an ontological foundation in the life of God. In the words of the Second Council of Constantinople (553), in Jesus Christ, do we encounter "unus de Trinitate"? Exactly this uniqueness is expressed in the concept of incarnation. God has placed himself under restriction by becoming human, as Patrick Lens aptly formulates.[25] For this reason we do not extend incarnational language to our exposition of the nature of the church; rather, we should use pneumatological language.

Trinity and the Personhood of the Spirit

In the light of the foregoing reflections, I draw the conclusion that attention to the Spirit in the life of Jesus will drastically reinterpret and correct classical Logos Christology. We are dealing with two models: one is an ascending model (Synoptic Gospels) and the other a descending model (the Gospel of John and Paul's letters). The descending, or return, model,

---

24. P. Lens, "God heeft zich aan onze menselijkheid gewaagd," *Comm* 21 (1996): 379.

25. Lens, "Schoonenberg en de uniciteit van Christus," 96.

on first sight, integrates the ascending model, but at the same time the ascending model maintains its own strength.

Either model in isolation from the other leads to one-sidedness. The best way to keep them together for contemporary theology and for the sake of the pastorate is to see them as complementary and reciprocal. The ascending Christology that speaks of Christ as anointed with the eschatological Spirit receives a further and decisive interpretation from the side of a descending Christology, or return model, because the latter articulates the unique anchoring of his Sonship in God. Also, the descending, or return, model is radically clarified by the ascending model because the latter makes undoubtedly clear that this person, the actual Jesus of Nazareth, was a Jew who lived in his times by the power of the Holy Spirit. Spirit Christology, which incorporates both an ascending and a descending model, enlightens and clarifies the inner dynamics by which the Sonship of Jesus is realized.

We thus cannot speak of the Logos or of preexistence apart from the story of Jesus Christ. The binding to this actual person and history implies that the concept of Logos cannot be understood in abstraction from the drama of salvation history of God and Israel. Logos cannot be defined a priori by properties that are deduced from our human limitations and boundaries, such as omniscience or omnipresence. The drama of the covenant between God and Israel, in which non-Jews are added by grace, should be taken seriously as the vantage point from which we confess who God is.

Of course, these considerations touch upon the theme of the cosmic Christ and his preexistence. What can we say about preexistence? Not so much! When in the Pauline letters and in the Gospel of John, Christ is confessed as already active

Toward a Sustainable Spirit-Christology

in creation,[26] from all eternity, this is the language of overwhelming surprise and praise of the richness of God. Systematic theology should help the reader of the Bible, the preacher, and every child of God affirm that surprise. We stand on the floor of history and are participants in that history, as well as recipients of that history; we do not have a place in the director's room. This means that constructive theological reflections should make space for two movements: one that walks along with the drama of the covenant, and one that looks back on the drama in light of the outcome.

Once again, what does such reflection mean for the preexistence of Christ and the immanent Trinity? Are these concepts only theological constructs, or do they present ontological content?

The church confesses that Jesus as the Son is begotten of the Father. That is, Jesus as an actually living and acting person is not strange to God, but in the deeds and person of Jesus, God confirms himself. He wants to have his name live on earth among his creatures, make himself present, and have justice and shalom be realized. The Old Testament pictured the encounter of God with Israel as a drama with several actors. It is a drama in which not only the people of Israel suffer by going in exile, but also God does not escape unhurt. In the mission of Jesus, God takes up the thread once more and confirms the goal of the covenant: "I will be your God and you will be my people." He confirms in the generation and mission of Jesus his own being in a way that had not occurred until then. In Chalcedon, this confirmation is expressed in terms of an assumption of the human nature: *assumptio carnis*. The meaning of the

---

26. 1 Corinthians 8:6; Ephesians 1:4; Colossians 1:16; John 1:1.

word *caro*, "flesh," must be broadened to include all that has been said. In the humanity of Jesus, God has bowed himself deeply to our seeking and longing life, in all its restrictedness, threat, and fragility, and has made it his own. In doing so, he affirms his divinity. That is his glory, the first thing we have to say about his divinity. All other things are secondary.

By confirmation, I mean that this movement of assumption is proper to God; it has its possibility in God himself. The appearance of this man Jesus in our history, in the time and space of this universe, finds its basic plan in God. That is, the relation of God the Father and Jesus Christ the Son has its presupposition or anchoring in who God is in his glory. The identification of Jesus with Word or Wisdom (Prov. 8) is not an invitation to speculate about a chronologically understood beginning but draws our thoughts to contemplate God's goal: to bring God's benevolence and love to its completion.[27] This focus is what the doctrine of preexistence wants to tell us. This man Jesus Christ and the kingdom he stands for is what God actually is and stands for. The togetherness of Father and Son, the benevolence that shines out from their relationship with each other, including in their conversation about us (see John 17), to which we are invited—these features are what and who God is in himself. Hence for Paul the confession of Israel, the Shema, can be reinterpreted christologically (1 Cor. 8:6). Here the proper ground of the uniqueness of Christ is laid bare. He partakes in the reign of God, and God is God in the unity of Father and this only Son.

In the terminology of classical Christology, we may thus say that the mystery of Jesus is that, in his life, God and man

---

27. Feldmeier and Spieckermann, *Der Gott der Lebendigen*, 255.

Toward a Sustainable Spirit-Christology

are together in a way that is in favor of us. This togetherness happens because of the assumption of our existence by God in the person of Jesus. It is not because of a natural susceptibility of our earthly being for divine being (*finitum non capax infiniti*) but only by way of God's graceful act (*infinitum capax finiti*). This assumption does not happen in a way that the order of our human being is changed or distorted but happens *secundum modum recipientis*; that is, the order of divine being subsists in the order of human being. Put otherwise, the divinity of Jesus is not something that stands on its own; rather, it is completely assumed and residing in that in which it subsists.[28]

In the language of the tradition, it means that the *enhypostasis* is in some way reversible. Not in the vein of Schoonenberg but in a sense that the human being and the divine being permeate each other. Not only does the humanity of Jesus find its center in the Word, but also the other way around: the Word fully subsists in and through the humanity of Jesus. Both orders are together but in such a way that the order of humanity is not removed.[29]

Two final questions: First, is it possible to say a bit more about the personality of the Spirit and the immanent Trinity? We operate on the edges of what can be said, but for theological reasons, something must be said. These are remarks on what the Christian community has received in the history of Israel and of Jesus. On the basis of that story, this much can be said: the Father generates the Son in the power of the Spirit, and the Son loves the Father in the power of the Spirit. The Spirit is the power bestowed by the Father on the Son, and the Spirit is the power by

---

28. Coffey, "Theandric Nature," 422.
29. Coffey, "Theandric Nature," 418.

which the Son is able to give himself completely to the Father. He is the anointed Son. In this formulation the Spirit is the principle of movement, opening, glorification, and communication.[30] This is also true for who God is in himself. The communication between Father and Son opens a new chapter, namely, our participation in the divine life, which aims toward the total transformation of the whole of our reality and universe. The Spirit is the eschatological reality and force in the divine life, by which God seeks the fulfillment and glorification of his works.

Second question: Is Christ an ordinary human being? Answer: Jesus is fully human but definitely not an ordinary human being. In him, God is with us. This sentence disrupts our horizon. Jesus's story is the *point* of history, but *still not* the full plot. The eschaton, the glorification, has happened to him in his exaltation but *not yet* to us. Jesus is resurrected in the eschaton, which is exactly what separates us from him. Where he is, we are *not yet*. Here the work of the Spirit is needed. If there is to be a bridge between Christ and us in this world of estrangement, it has to be built by the Spirit. Therefore another stage is opened: the outpouring of the Spirit and the calling of a community around Christ. It is the Spirit of the end time, this benevolent force, by which human beings become involved in God's grace and by which justice and shalom are forged.

30. "It is in that the Spirit is God as the Power of God's *own* and our future and, that is to say, the Power of a future that also for God is not bound by the predictabilities, that the Spirit is a distinct identity of and in God. The Spirit is God as his and our future rushing upon him and us; he is the eschatological reality of God, the Power as which God is the active Goal of all things, as which God is for himself and for us those 'things not seen' that with us call for faith and with him are his infinity" (Robert Jenson, *Systematic Theology*, vol. 1 [Oxford: Oxford University Press, 1997], 160).

4 God's Spirit as Transformative Power
Voices from the Reformed Tradition

Retaining the Transformative Power

Living in the West in the twenty-first century, when the sacred canopy is slowly melting away and when our societies seem to have become cynical about their own values and future, we may think that calling attention to the transformative power of the Holy Spirit is a hopeless task that is not worth much effort. I undertake this task anyway, not in the expectation that old cultural ideals will be restored to their former glory, but because of a theological imperative. If Christ reigns and his Spirit has been sent, then this world is not empty but has become the space in which Christ by his Spirit works and manifests himself against all resistance, breakdown, chaos, and death. In the New Testament, we read how the Spirit breaks through borders of language, land, culture, and gender, and how this exercises a corrective and transformative effect on people and their context by promoting an ethos of care, compassion, and humanity.

Nicholas Wolterstorff characterizes this ethos, as it became apparent in the Calvinism of the Puritans and in the theology of culture developed within neo-Calvinism, as "world formative Christianity."[1] In this chapter, I give attention to a few figures in whose thinking the Holy Spirit and his transformative influence on the believer, culture, and history are central: Calvin, Schleiermacher, and Kuyper. I do not choose them because they are the only ones that deserve recognition on this front; rather, they are representative. Other names such as Augustine, Jonathan Edwards, Frederick Denison Maurice, H. Richard Niebuhr, Wolfhart Pannenberg, Hendrikus Berkhof, and Arnold van Ruler could have been candidates as well. And why not also mention Karl Barth, who in *Christengemeinde und Bürgergemeinde* gave his interpretation to that great indicative in the Sermon on the Mount "You are the salt of the earth." More ominous, however, if not disastrous, is what follows next: "But if salt has lost its taste, how can its saltiness be restored?" (Matt. 5:13).

Calvin

Does John Calvin belong in this picture of world-formative Christianity? At first glance, he does not. Generally speaking, he held to a static view of society and regarded renewal as something bad. For a critical attitude against social institutions, most scholars point to later Calvinists. I nevertheless start with Calvin because of the impressive role that his the-

1. N. Wolterstorff, *Until Justice and Peace Embrace: The Kuyper Lectures for 1981, Delivered at the Free University of Amsterdam* (Grand Rapids: Eerdmans, 1983).

ology gives to the Holy Spirit as the force field of our life. In this force field, we are invited, indeed summoned, to give a response—to take up our responsibility. As recipients of God's gifts, believers are made into respondents and actors.

Warfield rightly called Calvin a theologian of the Holy Spirit. In Calvin's thought the Spirit has a comprehensive and structural meaning.[2] Perhaps the best way to get to know what the Spirit meant for Calvin is to look at what he wrote on the Holy Supper in his *Petit traicté de la Saincte Cene* (1541). The meal can be considered an intersection where various lines that are definitive for the existence of the believer visibly come together. Calvin sums up three functions. First, the Supper is primarily a gift through which God internalizes the promises that are contained in the gospel. The believer is an adopted child who enjoys a place and food at this table. Second, the table calls upon the faithful to acknowledge God's goodness toward them. The third function is related to the community: one who shares in the Supper is thereby included in the church and thus is called to a holy, purified life. Men and women are called to a response. Here, at the "welcome table,"[3] it becomes clear how important the Holy Spirit is for Calvin. The work of the Holy Spirit takes multiple forms. Not everything is accomplished in proclamation and faith. "For, first, the Lord teaches and trains us by his word; next, he confirms us by his sacraments; lastly, he illumines our mind by the light

2. See B. B. Warfield, *Calvin and Calvinism* (New York: Oxford University Press, 1931), 107, also his *Calvin and Augustine* (Philadelphia: Presbyterian & Reformed, 1956), 484.

3. Note the spiritual with the lines "I'm going to sit at the Welcome Table / Shout my troubles over / Walk and talk with Jesus."

of his Holy Spirit, and opens up an entrance into our hearts for his word and sacraments, which would otherwise only strike our ears, and fall upon our sight, but by no means affect us inwardly."[4] The Holy Spirit is "the internal Master, whose energy alone penetrates the heart, stirs up the affections, and procures access for the sacraments into our souls."[5] By the Holy Spirit, God comes near.

The activity of the Spirit, however, is not limited to the sphere of salvation but works in the cosmos and in history. Calvin did not live in our modern climate, where nature is regarded as dumb, a labyrinth of phenomena that must be mapped out bit by bit until the whole of reality lies open to our mind. On the contrary, for him nature was a reality that testified on all sides to a connection with its Creator. All things lay open to God's command. Medieval theology spoke in this respect of *potentia oboedentialis*. Calvin articulates this openness in terms of the Holy Spirit. The Spirit is the vital ground of being for everything that exists. It is notable that Calvin often speaks about the Spirit in terms of strength, power, influence, impulse, and instinct. This is power language.[6] God makes himself and his goodness visible, somehow tangible in the created world. Calvin often uses the metaphor of the mirror. God employs manifold mirrors to make himself known to the human being—in the created order, in the seasons, in rain and sun, but most of all in his Word, in Christ, and at the Holy Supper. These are all means in the hand of God, who wants

---

4. John Calvin, *Inst.* 4.14.8, https://www.ccel.org/ccel/calvin/insti tutes.vi.xv.html.

5. Calvin, *Inst.* 4.14.9.

6. W. Krusche, *Das Wirken des Heiligen Geistes nach Calvin* (Göttingen: Vandenhoeck & Ruprecht, 1957), 9.

Voices from the Reformed Tradition

to use all these elements to make his benevolence known to us and bring us to an obedient response.[7]

Calvin's theology is most fascinating because its pneumatology provides, on the one hand, a comprehensive theological framework with extensive attention to the universal action of the Spirit of God; on the other hand, it assigns the Spirit a decisive role in the relation of Christ to the believers. Both their union with Christ and their participation in the gifts of Christ are traced back to the power of the Spirit. Christ is never separated from his Spirit, as Calvin's axiom goes.[8] This principle becomes a pressing issue for explaining the Holy Supper, for since the ascension, Jesus Christ is at the right hand of God in heaven.

Calvin's vision of the ascension is fundamental to his theology and spirituality. The ascension is a strong caesura in the history of salvation. Since the ascension, Christ resides bodily in heaven in his glorified state as the mediator of redemption. Calvin is very decided in his opinion regarding the spatial determinacy and locality of this glorified physicality. He cannot imagine that the categorical terms of Christ's physicality undergo a change in Christ's glorification. The sharp debate with Joachim Westphal shows the difficulty of Calvin's position on this score. How could the distance between the heavenly Jesus Christ and the believer on earth be bridged? Calvin's view of the function of the Holy Spirit is essential here, for the Spirit bridges the gap. The Spirit is the activity of the triune God whereby eternal life and the power of the resurrection are

---

7. Cornelis van der Kooi, *As in a Mirror: John Calvin and Karl Barth on Knowing God; A Diptych* (Leiden: Brill, 2005), 77-80.

8. *CO* 49:491, commentary on 1 Corinthians 11:27.

now communicated to the faithful. Calvin does not espouse a real presence of the *body* of Christ in his account; rather, he stresses Christ's presence in his personal identity as mediator of salvation. Christ is present with respect to his comprehensive identity (*totus*) but not to everything (*non totum*) that belongs to his identity as mediator of redemption. To use an expression of Eberhard Jüngel, absence and presence are simultaneously together here, with the balance struck in favor of presence. And this surplus obtains on account of the Holy Spirit, who makes the power, the *virtus*, of Christ present in the Supper. It is the power of the Spirit that is constitutive of the presence of Christ.[9] By the power of the Spirit, we have communion with the body and blood of Christ.

This distinction is immediately related to the so-called *extra-calvinisticum*. Christ is related to creation and providence as the eternal Son and mediator of creation, and this cosmic activity and function continue when the eternal Son assumes human flesh. The cosmic activity of Christ as the eternal Son does not stop at the incarnation but is simultaneously working *extra carnem*. In Calvin's exposition of the ascension, this distinction once again becomes actual. On the one hand, Christ is the mediator of redemption, who is taken up into heaven with his human physicality; on the other hand, what belongs to his being continues to be active in the cosmos and history. This activity of the person of Christ is connected with the Spirit.

What is effected through that power of the Spirit? First, an actual transfer and transformation. The transfer is frequently described by Calvin as adoption—a legal and social

9. *CO* 48:12.

institution that was a familiar part of daily life in early sixteenth-century society, with its many orphans. The believer has the status of an adopted child and obtains a legal status, a place in the family—literally, a place at the table. Applied to the believer, this status means that we already experience, in part, eternal life here and now; we live in communion with Christ.

The indissolubility of this bond with Christ is of great, existential importance to Calvin. It worries him deeply when this communion with Christ seems to be jeopardized. The theory of soul sleep is therefore totally unacceptable to him.[10] He already fought against it before his transition to the Protestant camp was decided. It is an unbearable thought, completely at odds with his spirituality, that at some point the bond with the living Christ would be broken. People as pilgrims on their journey to the coming kingdom on earth already participate here and now in a hidden way in the salvation and the glory of God. This participation is the work of the Holy Spirit.

Adoption means much more, however. The adopted child must adjust to a new household, must learn a new style of living. Adoption implies the start of a lifelong transformation. It is telling in this connection that Calvin put so much emphasis on regeneration in the sense of sanctification, not least by discussing regeneration before justification.

What is the role of the Spirit *in* Christ? More specifically, what does his baptism or anointing with the Spirit do to Christ? As eternal Son, Christ already possesses all the full-

---

10. Cornelis van der Kooi, *As in a Mirror* (Leiden: Brill, 2005), 66n102.

ness of divinity. The baptism of Christ is therefore directed to his mission and office and is indissolubly related and limited to his human nature.[11] He does not need endowment with the Spirit for his divine nature. The restriction that Calvin makes is clear: everywhere during the life of Jesus, God's Spirit is at work, but the operation of the Spirit applies only to salvation for the people. In other words, Christ receives his anointing not so much for himself but for his friends, for the body of the church. Here the image of anointing turns out to have enormous potential for Calvin's theology and spirituality. Believers participate in all the goods that can be found in Christ by the Holy Spirit: "Then this anointing was diffused from the Head to the members, as Joel had foretold. . . . All who by faith perceive what he [Christ] is like have grasped the whole immensity of heavenly benefits."[12] In short, the glory of the exalted Lord has spread from him out to the church as his body and to each of its members. Huge potential lies in that image of anointing. Schleiermacher saw it, some of the liberal theologians made use of it, and it would be elaborated by Abraham Kuyper. I go a step further and would like to argue that this image provides us with possibilities to develop a pneumatology that helps us to be sensitive to the work of the Spirit, both in the church and in the culture.

For Calvin, anointing with the Holy Spirit has a strong eschatological thrust. The kingship of Christ is spiritual, remains mostly hidden, and will only later, in God's glory, come to true fulfillment. Participation in God's reign means that in all circumstances the believer remains under the protection

---

11. *CO* 45:126, commentary on Matthew 3:16.
12. Calvin, *Inst.* 2.15.2 (McNeill-Battles edition).

of Christ. God continues to care for his church through all the threats and dangers it encounters. In this context, Calvin recalls the gifts of the Spirit: wisdom, understanding, counsel and might, knowledge and fear of the Lord.[13] The Spirit is the good and blessed power of God by which he protects and encourages his children on their pilgrimage in this world. The work of the Spirit has duration and extension. Anointing points to a process, to a continued activity of God's Spirit.

I have long been intrigued by the word pair "Word and Spirit." This couplet plays a fundamental role in Calvin's doctrine of Scripture and also in what today is called spiritual formation and discernment. "Word" refers first of all to the concreteness of the Bible, to the sermon, and to Christ as the *Sermo Dei*. The Spirit is the inner teacher, the *magister interior*, who draws us toward the Word. Word and Spirit are two workings of God and cannot be reduced to one. They are to be regarded as two poles that make up the force field in which the believer is located. By Word and Spirit we are directed to Christ as the Mediator, who brings us into communion with God the Father. In the force field of Word and Spirit, we learn to discern the voice of the Good Shepherd. The Spirit has some independence in Calvin and is featured as a guide on his own. I quote John Hesselink:

> Calvin frequently points to a more common phenomenon and guidance in regard to the leading of the Spirit, i.e. that all believers can anticipate—providing they seek God's help with the right attitude—a special guidance of the Spirit in making various kinds of judgments and de-

13. See Calvin, *Inst.* 2.15.5 (McNeill-Battles edition), 499.

cisions. Accordingly, when David prays "teach me that I may do thy will," Calvin interprets this request as for something far more than seeking deliverance, but what is of still greater importance, viz., the guidance of God's Spirit, that he might not deviate to the right hand or the left, but be kept in the path of rectitude.[14]

Aiming at a further development of Reformed pneumatology and its associated spirituality, we should identify the means of grace more broadly than with sermons and sacraments. I have already mentioned that in Calvin the mirrors in which God makes himself visible are not restricted to the Bible and the sermon. The means that the Holy Spirit employs are diverse and polyphonic. Today we need to get a new awareness for this polyphony and diversity in the work of the Spirit. I am convinced that the word pair "Word and Spirit" offers an important possibility for developing a theology that fosters a spirituality that is sensitive to the work of the Spirit. The experience of the charismatic renewal within Protestant churches can benefit such a theology.

The means of the Spirit cannot be reduced to preaching and definitely not to intellectual understanding. Such a reduction has often happened, for example, in the nineteenth century by Ferdinand C. Baur and Alexander Schweizer when they drew upon Reformed theology and spirituality through the sieve of German idealism. Their retrieval of Reformed theology was in many respects grand and impressive, but it

14. See I. John Hesselink, "Governed and Guided by the Spirit: A Key Issue in Calvin's Doctrine of the Holy Spirit," in *Reformiertes Erbe: Festschrift für Gottfried W. Locher*, ed. H. A. Oberman, vol. 2 (Zürich: Theologischer Verlag, 1993), 168.

functioned also as a "dehumidifier" that removed all suppleness from the material and left it dried out and crumpled up. Historically, this process resulted in an enormous desiccation of spirituality. In the theology and spirituality that can be found in Calvin himself, formed as he was in the atmosphere of the *Devotio Moderna* of Thomas à Kempis and Geert Grote, sensory perception played an essential role. Not only is hearing important, but also the eye draws the human being toward the majesty of God found in the cosmos, the stars, the regularity of the seasons, and the cycles of day and night. In Calvin, all such phenomena remain tokens of God's benevolence that God has displayed for the godly and ungodly alike to see. The avenue of the Spirit runs from outside to inside and from the inside to above. The Eucharist, or Holy Supper, is not a bare meal of remembrance, which boils down to an intellectual exercise, but is an event that involves the senses. Calvin himself explicitly states that the Holy Supper is definitely more than a cognitive aid. But these sorts of notions were lost quickly in the history of Reformed spirituality and only later rediscovered by John W. Nevin (1803-86).[15]

Calvin's thoughts on the Holy Spirit and human pilgrimage reflect a strong eschatological perspective. The eye trained by the Spirit is focused on the heavenly homeland, on the future with Christ. The anointing of the Spirit feeds endurance, patience, faith, and wisdom. The transformation, however, also has an effect on the wider community. Gratefulness for all the gifts of God stirs up a reaction from our side. We are called to sanctification, to renewal day by day. And this call to

15. John W. Nevin, *Mystical Presence: A Vindication of the Reformed or Calvinistic Doctrine of the Eucharist* (Philadelphia: Fisher, 1846).

sanctification remains not only personal for Calvin; it could also mean an appeal to justice for the government, kings, and rulers. In other words, the transformative spirituality of Calvin's theology fostered, together with other societal factors, a transformative Christianity.

Schleiermacher

As a second example of a theology, in this case a full-blown Spirit Christology, with strong transformative features, I consider that of Friedrich Schleiermacher. Formally, Schleiermacher follows traces of the Reformed tradition with a concept of Spirit that encompasses the whole of his thought. He tries to develop a concept of Spirit that not only reinterprets traditional pneumatology but relates pneumatology to the philosophical concept of spirit of his time.[16]

It is extremely fascinating to see how, already in his youth, Schleiermacher develops notions that return in his mature theology. The natural tendency of the human spirit is that it strives to become self-transparent and in so doing gets to know its own freedom and essence. It is essential that the activity of the human spirit always goes through polarities, such as the contradiction between outside and inside, thinking and acting, receptivity and spontaneity, and assimilation

---

16. Martin Diederich, *Schleiermachers Geistverständnis: Eine systematisch-theologische Untersuchung seiner philosophischen und theologischen Rede von Gott* (Göttingen: Vandenhoeck & Ruprecht, 1999), 341; Ilka Werner, *Calvin und Schleiermacher im Gespräch mit der Weltweisheit: Das Verhältnis von christlichem Wahrheitsanspruch und allgemeinem Wahrheitsbewusstsein* (Neukirchen: Neukirchener Verlag, 1999), 276-78.

and externalization. In that oscillating movement between these polarities, the human spirit is a progressive power that brings reality to its highest unity. The spirit is thus the active power in a comprehensive process of culture and history. But exactly in striving toward that goal, natural consciousness reaches a limit that it cannot transcend. In the story of the human spirit, a deficit shows up, an inability.[17] An ideal of fulfillment shines through, but the human being is not able to bring it about. From a religious-philosophical perspective, the highest fulfillment can be thought of only as a new creative moment. Schleiermacher did not think of this new creative moment as something that in its own power could come into being within the natural context. It can be thought of only as a new beginning from the side of God. This new element has become real in the life of Jesus. Schleiermacher thus supposes in the connection between a general ontology and Christian pneumatology a turn that does not arise from history itself.

Low or High Christology?

Schleiermacher's pneumatology first becomes concrete in his Christology, which is explicitly a Spirit Christology. The divine in Jesus is the Spirit of God, which develops itself in Jesus as a complete God-consciousness. This fact does not find its explanation from any preceding history of humanity. In Schleiermacher's words, "That is, [Jesus's] distinctive

17. Friedrich Schleiermacher, *Christian Faith*, trans. Terrence N. Tice, Catherine L. Kelsey, and Edwina Lawler, vol. 2 (Louisville: Westminster John Knox, 2016), 403.

spiritual content cannot be accounted for based only on the content of the circle of human beings to which he belonged. Rather, it can be accounted for based only on the general source of spiritual life through a creative divine act, in which act the concept of the human being as the subject who holds God-consciousness is completed to an absolutely greatest extent."[18] In the light of such clear statements, the judgment of Karl Barth that Schleiermacher substituted anthropology for theology must be regarded as incorrect.

What kind of Christology is this actually? Is it high or low? All in all, Schleiermacher presents a high Christology that, in its own way, preserves the particularity and uniqueness of Jesus Christ.[19] Before Christ there is an insufficiency of God's Spirit, but in Jesus himself there reigned, "by the steady strength of his God-consciousness," a strength "that was an actual being of God in him."[20] All utterances of Jesus, the whole of his psychological activity, can be traced back to an impulse of God's Spirit.

Ecclesiology and Pneumatology

Schleiermacher's pneumatology becomes concrete in his ecclesiology. The way in which the Spirit is realized in Jesus

18. Schleiermacher, *Christian Faith*, 569.
19. See K. W. Hector, "Actualism and Incarnation: The High Christology of Friedrich Schleiermacher," *International Journal for Systematic Theology* 8 (2006): 307-22; and Bruce L. McCormack, "Über Barth hinaus—mit Schleiermacher?," in *Karl Barth und Friedrich Schleiermacher: Zur Neubestimmung ihres Verhältnisses*, ed. M. Gockel and M. Leiner (Göttingen: Vandenhoeck & Ruprecht, 2015), 79-86.
20. Schleiermacher, *Christian Faith*, 574.

immediately influences those who are with him. This influence comes by the communication of the Spirit, and by the Spirit's self-communication people come to their highest self-awareness. Right from the start, the Spirit is something communal. Schleiermacher relates the Spirit first of all to the community and only secondarily to the individual. The Spirit generates a communal activity in which the members of the community make the Spirit actual and present to each other, and in this way, the community shares the Spirit. This communality, intersubjectivity, and productive dialectic between community and individual is one of the significant features of Schleiermacher's dialogue "Weihnachtsfeier" (1806), a novella. The productive function of the intersubjectivity is the ground of the emergence and the continuity of faith communities. The Spirit reigning in these communities is called the "common spirit" (*Gemeingeist*).[21]

These notions exercised a deep influence on nineteenth-century Christian thought, not the least on neo-Calvinism, as can be perceived in the theology of culture of Abraham Kuyper and Herman Bavinck. In Schleiermacher's theology the Spirit moves in a linear way through history, taking

21. Schleiermacher, *Christian Faith*: "Consistent with what was indicated above, the term 'Holy Spirit' is understood to mean the unity of life that is inherent in Christian community, viewed as a moral person. Moreover, since everything that is actually law-bound is already excluded from it, we would be able to designate this presence in terms of the 'common spirit' of that community" (§116, p. 765). Regarding the communication of the Holy Spirit, Schleiermacher writes: "All who are living in the state of sanctification are conscious of an inner drive to become increasingly at one in a common cooperative and mutually interactive existence, this driving force being viewed as the common spirit of the new collective life founded by Christ" (heading to §121, pp. 796-97).

possession of communities. Thus the Spirit becomes disconnected from the historical Jesus and becomes an active gestalt on its own, communicating itself by its own power and with infinite variety. This *Gemeingeist* surfaces in the intersubjectivity that inspires and qualifies every member of the community. In this pneumatology intersubjectivity is basic and is connected with Schleiermacher's strong emphasis on—as Michael Welker puts it—the context sensitivity and polyphony of the Holy Spirit.[22] The oneness of the Spirit articulates itself in a plenitude of external, visible, and empirical data, always related to context. The members of this community distinguish themselves by an endless variety of relationships with each other. By the Spirit, a common feeling and cohesion is built up in family life, school, and state. Out of this awareness of mutual belonging, new spontaneous action can emerge that is of profit for the whole community.[23]

This idea of a communal spirit in which each member participates immediately signals the democratizing potential of Schleiermacher's pneumatology. It fostered the rising democratic tendencies of the nineteenth century. It can prompt us to a fresh reflection on the work of the Spirit if we are to

---

22. At the end of the eighteenth century, the meaning of the concept "spirit" became detached from its relation to the individual subject, and more Old Testament-related and vitalistic aspects of meaning were absorbed. "Spirit" became the designation of a founding and creative center of social formation like family, society, city, and state. Already with Nicholas Zinzendorf, we find the concept "Gemeingeist," that is, the spirit that dwells in a community of people and that imbues, activates, and mobilizes it. See Dorothee Schlenke, *Geist und Gemeinschaft: Die systematische Bedeutung der Pneumatologie für Friedrich Schleiermachers Theorie der christlichen Frömmigkeit* (Berlin: de Gruyter, 1999), 319-21, 326-33.

23. Schlenke, *Geist und Gemeinschaft*, 344-51.

Voices from the Reformed Tradition

rethink the work of the Spirit and ecclesiology in our own time. It was the young Abraham Kuyper who picked up this democratic potential and elaborated it socially, culturally, and politically.

Schleiermacher's pneumatology can in no way be accused of a narrow individualism, as was later the case with the pneumatology of the Holiness Movement and classical Pentecostal theology. The gift of the Spirit is, as in the book of Acts, an event that affects the community. In being focused on each other, in having impact on each other, and in mutual relationship, a common awareness comes into being in which the Spirit is fully present. In this way, the individual person is absorbed by the society, which by this process of distinction and interrelationship grows increasingly into the one body of Christ. To use another popular concept of Schleiermacher, this body is an organism that by itself effects and influences power. Fundamentally, unity and diversity go together.[24]

Schleiermacher gave form to this polyphonic character and context sensitivity of the Spirit in his "Weihnachtsfeier."[25] This tale describes a family, accompanied by some friends, gathering on Christmas Eve for a united celebration of Christmas. Every member in this circle is connected with the whole and is able to contribute something. Small children and women are definitely included in the mutual exchange

24. Schleiermacher, *Christian Faith*, "Since the divine being is but *one* being, everywhere self-identical, even though the way God exists in the individual being of Christ and in the collective life of the church is not the same, nevertheless, in the two cases the impetus that proceeds from the divine being can only be that which we have named" (§125.1, p. 819).

25. Schleiermacher, "Die Weihnachtsfeier: Ein Gespräch" (1806), in *Schriften aus der Hallenser Zeit, 1804-1807*, ed. Hermann Patsch, vol. 1.5 of *Kritische Gesamtausgabe* (Berlin: de Gruyter, 1995), 39-98.

and participation in this community. Differences between men and women, old and young, married and unmarried, and differences in musical and mental capacities do not hinder or destroy the upbuilding of the whole but make visible and tangible the wealth of the various aspects of the divine Spirit. In this picture of a community in which everybody has a share in God's Spirit and contributes something to the wellbeing of the whole, there becomes visible not only a strong democratic tendency but also something resonant with the prophecy of Joel 3. Women, children, old, and young will be prophets of the kingdom.

Kingdom of God and Society

From this point it can be understood that, in line with Schleiermacher's pneumatology, a concept of the kingdom of God can be developed that takes its point of departure from the common life of the religious community. The Holy Spirit is immanent in human nature and strives to permeate and appropriate this nature. This intention is not restricted to individual persons, however, but aims by its communal character at the whole human community, that is to say, at the culture as a whole. This communal dynamic of the Spirit finds its goal and completion in the concept of the kingdom of God. It belongs to the self-movement of the Spirit that it strives to absorb all other functions of human consciousness. The whole of natural life, with its many psychological and cultural articulations, becomes in this way an organ and means for the realization of the Spirit of God. Schleiermacher presupposes a kind of susceptibility or openness to the Holy Spirit in all humans. Natural life possesses a receptivity to the prospect of being completed by the Holy Spirit; so also are the other natural, affective, psychic, and spiritual faculties. Flesh and sin are not regarded as rebelling against God but as the still-existing and not-yet-conquered autonomy of natural-rational life.

Christianity does not stand square upon human culture; rather, human culture is presupposed by Christianity. From this perspective the cultural, political, pedagogical, and ethical ideals of Schleiermacher can be understood. The dominance of the divine consciousness realized in Jesus Christ must realize itself from now on in all spheres of life as a moral impulse by which all acts of the members of this communal life are determined by this communal spirit as "the innermost impulse of the individual."[26] In other words, Christianity will bring into being a totally Christian culture. On this very point, Barth will follow a totally different path.

Kuyper

Schleiermacher's view of Christianity as a transformative power of church and society becomes even more distinctive with Abraham Kuyper, a conclusion that holds true for the whole of his career as a theologian, journalist, and statesman. I first make a few comments about the early Kuyper and his view on church and society. Among the options regarding the relationship of church and state that were available around the middle of the nineteenth century, three stood out. First,

26. Schleiermacher, *Christian Faith*, §116.3, p. 766.

there was a movement inspired by Hegel that regarded the state as the fulfillment of the moral ideal that lives within humanity. Second, there was a neo-orthodox group that defended the church as the institution of salvation. Third, there was a group inspired by Schleiermacher, for whom the church existed "by way of voluntary fellowship and mutual cooperation of regenerate people. Here the free forming of a societal community comes first and foremost, under the influence of the one Spirit of the Christ and independent of the state."[27] In his prize-winning *Commentatio* of 1861, which compared the ecclesiology of Calvin and Johannes à Lasco, Kuyper shows a clear preference for the thought of the Polish noble à Lasco precisely because of his ecclesiology. Calvin's ecclesiology, by Kuyper's lights, was too hierarchically structured; à Lasco's was more democratic.

Kuyper was a student of Schleiermacher in these early years. He emphasizes the social element in Schleiermacher's ideas. For Kuyper, the church is not so much determined by public ceremonies or by confessional agreement but by communion. Christ is the central cogwheel that sets all the other parts in motion. All the members of the congregation partake in the Holy Spirit. Kuyper uses the word "organism" as a tool to point to the priesthood of all believers and to the leadership of those who are more advanced in faith and love.[28] "Organism" was also the word used to resolve the tension between the individual and society. This word shows the influence of

---

27. See J. Vree and J. Zwaan, "Historical Introduction," in *Introduction, Annotation, Bibliography, and Indices*, vol. 1 of *Abraham Kuyper's Commentatio (1860): The Young Kuyper about Calvin, a Lasco, and the Church* (Leiden: Brill, 2005), 14.

28. Kuyper, *Commentatio*, 303-4.

Schleiermacher and Kuyper's knowledge of Schleiermacher's *Christian Faith*.[29] The consequences of the idea of the church as organism came to the fore in the young Kuyper's career, particularly on the matter of leadership. Whereas other leading theologians in the Netherlands considered the masses still too uneducated to vote for elders and deacons, Kuyper regarded all the members of the community as capable of voting.[30] He also included women. He not only awarded them the right to vote but even made them eligible for the position of deacon.[31] With this stance, Kuyper's career in national politics was launched.

This plea for a moderate democracy was clearly in opposition to the current "dominocracy," or the dominating role of ministers in the church. Kuyper's vision for his country becomes manifest: the church as a community will show its stature and will exert its efforts for the good of the society. Its emphasis should therefore be on mission; out there is a world to be won. The famous quote of Kuyper concerning the lordship of Jesus Christ over "every square inch" can already be found in this youthful work. The whole human race is the domain of the church; for this reason, even the very smallest part cannot remain untouched, until every knee should bow at the name of Jesus.[32]

Kuyper used the doctrine of the sovereignty of God as

29. See Schleiermacher, *Christian Faith*, 753.
30. Kuyper, *Commentatio*, §194, 344.
31. Vree and Zwaan, *Introduction, Annotation, Bibliography, and Indices*, 60.
32. Kuyper, *Commentatio*, 363: "Universum humanum genus ecclesiae est dominium, quapropter ne vel tantillum intactum est relinquendum donec in nomine Iesu flectatur omne genu."

a crowbar to open the closed doors of a class-ridden society in which the masses were fenced off from education, voting rights, and health care. Later, in his 1874 lecture "Calvinism: Source and Stronghold of Our Constitutional Liberties," Kuyper points to the absolute sovereignty of God as the foundation of all power. God's sovereignty implies that no power on earth is inherent; rather, all power is delegated by God. "Only God is sovereign; He regards all creatures, whether born in royal palace or beggar's hut, as nothing in comparison with Himself."[33] Following from this confession of God's sovereignty comes the doctrine of election. But far from warranting fatalism or passivity, this doctrine in Kuyper's theology turns out to be a tool of mobilization. From the same lecture: "Whoever believes in election, knows that he has been chosen for something, that this is a spiritual calling, and that, as a divine calling, it may require the dearest sacrifice. At the same time, it is a calling that guarantees success. Since God is the sovereign who calls him, he does not hesitate, does not weigh the pros and cons, but takes hold of the job and perseveres."[34] Kuyper provided his generation with a comprehensive vision of the history and goal of the universe. By doing so, he fueled his generation with hope and mobilized those who had heretofore stayed outside the mainstream of modernizing society.

What can we retain from Kuyper's concepts in our own time, and what should be reconsidered? At the very least, Kuyper provided his church and society with a pneumatology that gave more attention to the sustaining work of the

33. Translation taken from James Bratt, *Abraham Kuyper: A Centennial Reader* (Grand Rapids: Eerdmans, 1998), 307.
34. Bratt, *Abraham Kuyper*, 309-10.

Spirit in Jesus. As I see it, he elaborates this aspect deeper than Calvin did. The Spirit initiated development in the life of Jesus and sustained him in his humanity.[35] The eternal Son assumed a human nature that was not sinful but nevertheless was weakened because of the effects of sin. Though rejecting any thought of inner contagion, Kuyper nevertheless deemed the Spirit to be necessary to elevate Jesus's "sunken" human nature and to bring it to glory. The Holy Spirit is the one who endowed Jesus with the most delightful gifts, powers, and faculties of which human nature is capable.[36]

Kuyper's exposition of the concept of anointing shows something of his high expectations for human beings and human faculties. Human nature is so constituted that it is susceptible to the influence and gifts of the Holy Spirit, which implies an openness for the gifts of the Spirit in principle. What the Spirit did to the human nature of Jesus Christ—elevating, endowing, and empowering—can be expected to be the future for every human being.[37] Our world and cosmos are not at all empty; they are no product of blind fate but serve to make visible the glory of God. What happens to us in the place and time where we live is part of a bigger picture and has already been decided in God's eternal council. Onward to that goal the Spirit drives this world, but this process takes time. Kuyper, never in want of images and metaphors, points to the contemporary construction of the water-supply system

35. Abraham Kuyper, *The Work of the Holy Spirit* (1888; Grand Rapids: Eerdmans, 1975), 93-96.

36. Kuyper, *The Work of the Holy Spirit*, 95.

37. Abraham Kuyper, *Het werk van de Heilige Geest* (Kampen: Kok, 1927), 157. The English translation turns out to give a summary of the original Dutch and misses the crucial statement.

in the city of Rotterdam. First, the system for the city will be completed, and then the system for the village of Feyenoord; only when these systems are done can the water supply reach the outer suburbs as well.[38] This is how he looks at the history of Europe over against the development of the people of Asia and Africa. They all would finally profit from development, from the ongoing work of the Spirit, but it would take time. Kuyper's concept still operated within the borders of a Eurocentric and Western outlook, but his vision was worldwide.

There is, however, a typical and, in my opinion, dangerous structural duality in this theology that we already found in Calvin: the sharp distinction, if not separation, between the universal activity of Christ and the Spirit, on the one hand, and on the other, the saving activity of Christ and the Spirit. Both operations have their foundation in God's eternal council. The eternal perspective of God's council gives Kuyper the opportunity to develop a grand vision of the whole history and fate of the human race and cosmos. What Kuyper later, in the years 1895-1901, developed under the denominator of common grace can already be found *in nuce* in *The Work of the Holy Spirit*. There is first a general or universal working of the Spirit by which God touches and empowers all created being; second, there is the saving activity of the Spirit. The gifts and workings of this universal Spirit have their effects in the arts, in labor, in invention, and in the development of science and culture. So when a sick person goes to a medical doctor, though the doctor may not be a believer at all, even a despiser of church and God, the person is consulting someone who is unwittingly and unwillingly a tool of the

---

38. Kuyper, *The Work of the Holy Spirit*, 123.

Voices from the Reformed Tradition

Spirit of God. On the ground of common grace the whole of modern culture with its achievements and potential must be embraced as a gift and work of the eternal God. Modern society, medical advancement, and new laws for social justice are to be seen as means in the hand of God, who combats evil and who drives his world to its final goal—that is, the regeneration of the universe. Regeneration is thus not only a concept that has to do with the "saved" person but is related to God's goal for creation as a whole. Kuyper used the Greek word *palingenesis* ("rebirth") in his address "The Blurring of the Boundaries" (1892) as counterpart to the modern idea of evolution. Instead of evolution, the church should embrace the vision of the regeneration of God's creation. He writes: "A life-sphere of our own on the foundation of *palingenesia* and a life-view of our own thanks to the light that the Holy Spirit kindles on the candelabra of Scripture. Not in the least, then, a passive group of pious mystics, but our own principle for our own higher learning, deriving from that principle our own conviction, and seeking to apply that conviction to life in all its rich fullness."[39] This grand vision functioned as an admonition to his followers not to stay apart from society but to participate in it actively and to harvest the fruits as gifts of God's benevolence.

Evaluation and Conclusion

I briefly note some achievements and also the shadow side of this vision. I mention both because we still live in these shad-

39. "The Blurring of the Boundaries," in Bratt, *Abraham Kuyper*, 400.

ows; we have become more aware of them from the encounter of traditional Western Christianity with world Christianity. In the first place, modernization and progress are regarded as outworkings of God's eternal council, which function in neo-Calvinistic theology as reason to engage fully in modern culture. This effect can be regarded as also theologically positive: this world and its potentialities are in principle part of God's creation and should be brought under the dominion of Christ's lordship. It even links up with the famous saying of Schleiermacher that the knot of history should not boil down to Christian faith with barbarism and science with unbelief. But we have to mention here also a possible shadow of this ethos: Do we have to say that Kuyper's vision of common grace and palingenesis also resulted in a complete surrender to modernity?

Second, this view of the universal working of the Spirit fosters indirectly the medicalization of the body within the church. The development of medical science can be accepted and hailed as an effect of common grace. This view can easily result in a kind of everyday dualism. For one's body, one goes to the doctor; for one's soul, to the church. But are health and sickness not something that should also belong within the faith community? Charismatic spirituality can be seen as a critical countermovement.

Third, and in connection with this point: What is the place of prayer in this kind of theology? For Kuyper, prayer was finally adjusting your heart and will to the eternal will and council of God, with the goal of finding rest in his good pleasure. But does Scripture really teach such a view of prayer? When Jesus prayed in the garden of Gethsemane, his prayer sounded rather different.

And a fourth and even more theological shadow I wish to point to is the following: Is it possible to make such a split between the various workings of the Spirit? If the Spirit is the Spirit of the triune God, can the work of the Spirit then be divided into such neat sectors? Should we not hold to the unity of God's Spirit? The Spirit is the Spirit of the Son of the Father, which means that no evidence of the Spirit's work can be thought to exist completely outside the orbit of the Father's incredible benevolence. There may be distinctions in the works of the Spirit, but it is the same Spirit of the Son of the Father.

What can we get from this idea of God's Spirit as transformative power? Or has this branch of Reformed theology gone too far, become too optimistic? Is it simply a vision too this-worldly, too triumphalistic? Of course, it is optimistic and tends to triumphalism. It reflects a time in which Europe and the United States regarded themselves as cultures inspired and molded by the impact of God's Spirit, by the leaven of the gospel. The awareness that salt can lose its taste, and in fact may have lost its taste on many occasions, or even that the salt was never there, sharpened in our hearts and minds over the course of the twentieth century. I know many theologians who are of the opinion that this kind of thought—Christ or the Spirit of Christ as transformer of culture—must be abandoned. The critical voices of the young Karl Barth, John Howard Yoder, Stanley Hauerwas, and my colleague Bram van de Beek, to mention only a few, are clear.

But is that all that needs to be said? Should we retreat to the thought of church as counterculture and surrender the world to the world? At least, I want to say that we are left with the command of Jesus for the new community: "You are the salt of the earth." The next question is how this salt works in our lives and communities, in our institutions, in our way of doing theology. Reformed theology has as its center the proclamation of the gospel and the administration of the sacraments. At the Supper, God's welcome table, God's hospitality in Christ is celebrated and a new ethos is promoted, forthcoming from the experience of the gift. This ethos in the Reformed tradition is connected with the metaphor of anointing. The participants at the table are told that they somehow share in this anointing and that the fruits of this anointing can be expected to become manifest.

5 The Threefold Office
Criterion for Living the Christian Life

Unused Wiring

Some houses have electrical wiring installed throughout the place, only to be capped with a cover plate instead of an actual socket. As a result, the wiring actually remains unused. I wonder whether this analogy might describe the situation regarding the metaphor of anointing as it is found in Calvin's doctrine of the threefold office of Christ[1] and taken up in the Reformed confessions. It is a pneuma metaphor that offers rich possibilities for bridging the gap between Christ and us, between Christology and pneumatology. Here I cite only the Heidelberg Catechism, which indeed draws a very direct connection between Christ and believers—in the very context of the name "Christ" no less!

> *Question 31: Why is He called Christ, that is, Anointed?*
> Because He has been ordained by God the Father, and anointed with the Holy Spirit, to be our chief Prophet and

---

1. For example, see Calvin, *Inst.* 2.15.

Teacher, who has fully revealed to us the secret counsel and will of God concerning our redemption; our only High Priest, who by the one sacrifice of His body has redeemed us, and who continually intercedes for us before the Father; and our eternal King, who governs us by His Word and Spirit, and who defends and preserves us in the redemption obtained for us.

Question 32: Why are you called a Christian?

Because I am a member of Christ by faith and thus share in His anointing, so that I may as prophet confess His Name, as priest present myself a living sacrifice of thankfulness to Him, and as king fight with a free and good conscience against sin and the devil in this life, and hereafter reign with Him eternally over all creatures.

My interest is not in precisely what the authors of the catechism themselves meant with the anointing image but in the effects of the anointing made concrete for us by using the threefold office. This is interesting in view of the discussion in this series of lectures. The anointing image has enormous consequences: the same Spirit with whom Jesus was baptized, who came upon him and made him the revelation of God's love, has also been poured out over his followers and over his church. This action is quite something, since it now focuses the spotlight on the Christian church and on believers. We are already *within* the reach of the Spirit, and as a result we become active as subjects. What has been given in Jesus calls for a creative response in a multitude of lives, circumstances, places, and times. In the preceding chapter we encountered the question of the wider, cultural effects: are the effects of the Spirit visible in the wider community, in politics, in trade unions, in sports, and in your own home? The question I now turn to is how and where these effects can be seen. To that end I would like to use the doctrine of the threefold office as a theological tool. Just like a GPS module can show us where we are, so the doctrine of the threefold office can function as a Global Positioning System to determine our place and course.

Spirit and Office

The doctrine of the threefold office offers a way to expand Christology pneumatologically with a view to relevant issues pertaining to church and worship, the relationship between Christian faith and ethics, justice, culture, the gifts of grace, and, for example, the issue of prayer and healing. In all cases the question is how God is present in our world through his Spirit in order to save, heal, support, transform, and bless.

Using the concept of the threefold office makes it possible to reenergize classical Christology with its dual schemes. I follow here Heiko A. Oberman, who stated that Calvin's use of the doctrine of the threefold office marks the transition from a two-natures Christology to a more functional Christology.[2] The doctrine of the two natures is not rejected or dropped, but it receives a new dynamic, more in line with what the one person Jesus Christ did. In this line, it is also possible to reinterpret the doctrine of the so-called *extra-calvinisticum*—that is, to reener-

2. H. A. Oberman, "Die 'Extra'-Dimension in der Theologie Calvins," in *Die Reformation: Von Wittenberg nach Genf* (Göttingen: Vandenhoeck & Ruprecht, 1986), 276.

gize it as well. This doctrine articulates the conviction that God himself is at work in differing avenues and modes. In creation, it is God who creates this world, and it is this very God who in the history of Israel acts, steers, corrects, and liberates.[3] He does so by giving the Ten Commandments, by sending the angels and the angel of the Lord, by dwelling in the temple, and by settling his name in Jerusalem. It is all aimed at the life-giving presence and saving nearness of this one God. The question of the saving nearness of God gets a final and decisive answer in the mission of Jesus Christ. In him, God becomes Immanuel and makes his name dwell on the earth. In him, God says Yes to his covenant with Abraham (2 Cor. 1:19-20). For that reason the identity of this person and his work can be described in Acts 10:38 in terms of Spirit: "for God was with him." I therefore join Barth in his criticism of the separation of traditional theology between Christ as creation Mediator and Christ as salvation Mediator. The distinction between God the Eternal Son and God the incarnate Son leads to separation in the person of the Logos or the Son. The doctrine of the two natures has provided the spectacles for such a reading, by which the rift in the concept of the Son was finally sealed. That is, it is easy to "know" of the eternal Son in a way that lacks sufficient grounding in the biblical texts. The texts that are traditionally regarded as the *dicta probantia* for the Creator mediatorship of the eternal Son are spoken in relation to a view of the earthly Jesus on his way to the cross and then exalted. They are doxological sayings in

3. Cornelis van der Kooi, "The Identity of Israel's God: The Potential of the So-Called Extra-Calvinisticum," in *Tradition and Innovation in Biblical Interpretation: Studies Presented to Professor Eep Talstra on the Occasion of His Sixty-Fifth Birthday*, ed. W. T. van Peursen and J. W. Dyk (Leiden: Brill, 2011), 209-22.

view of this one figure, who made God's kingdom present. This very man Jesus is the glorious linchpin in the plot of history, the key of the universe. He was in a mysterious way already always in the game and part of it. And now this rule of the Crucified One is proclaimed as everlasting. That is what these texts tell. But something different will be the result when these doxological texts are read against the background of a doctrine of two natures—namely, that by doing so, a separation is made in the work and person of this one person Jesus Christ. To say it boldly: we know of the preexistent Son only in the mirror of his concrete existence as earthly person and through his post-earthly existence as glorified and exalted Son. Preexistence articulates that it is God himself who becomes present in Jesus as the Son. The confession of the *sessio ad dexteram* tells us that the exalted and glorified Jesus partakes as the Son in the rule of God the Father.

The work and person of Christ are examined through the lens of the three functions according to which God had already been present among his people: prophet, priest, and king. What is remarkable about the Heidelberg Catechism is participation in Christ being expressed in terms of anointing or baptism with the Spirit. Our union with Christ and participation in his work are then formulated as participation in baptism with that same Holy Spirit. In all of this, our dependence on Christ remains fundamental and untouched. It is Christ who sends the Spirit. Ever since the Son was glorified, there is no Spirit of God who is not at the same time the Spirit of the Son of the Father. Our participation is not formulated in terms of incarnation, but the language used is purposely pneumatological. I briefly elaborate here the difference between a christological perspective and a pneumatological perspective.

Participation in the Spirit of Christ

The nature of our participation in salvation differs, depending on whether it is viewed from a christological or from a pneumatological perspective.[4] There are structural differences between the two. When we are called children of God and declared to be righteous, this wording implies a soteriological act on the part of God for human beings. It is something that takes places outside of us, *extra nos*; it comes to pass by a word that comes to us from God. We are altogether passive in this act. His Yes establishes our union with Christ. As such, the concept of justification marks the step by which God reconquers the world for himself. To use the terms of Lord's Day 1 of the catechism, this action means that we "belong" to Christ. It is our adoption and involves nothing less than a transfer. In contrast, sanctification, or renewal, differs structurally from justification. In sanctification an indwelling (*inhabitatio*) of the Spirit takes place; something occurs in us. This is a momentous realization. We participate as subjects, are activated as agents. The Spirit's indwelling does not, of course, lead to deification, to a unicity that in the context of Christology came to be expressed by the terms "hypostatic union" and enhypostasis. We do not have the unique relationship with God that Christ enjoyed. We are God's *adopted* children. Yet this status in itself is a great mystery: it is the triune God who dwells in us, who has poured out his Spirit in his church! At the same time, this indwelling is not a matter of peace but

4. Arnold A. van Ruler, "Structural Differences between the Christological and the Pneumatological Perspectives," in his *Calvinist Trinitarianism and Theocentric Politics: Essays towards a Public Theology*, trans. and ed. John Bolt (Lewiston, NY: Edwin Mellen, 1989), 27-46.

Criterion for Living the Christian Life

involves warfare. We are often stubborn and do not readily incline to the Spirit and his work. In fact, the Holy Spirit may be grieved and even snuffed out. The house may feel or even be empty. Before we know it, we may be overcome by what in the monastic tradition is called the demon of acedia. It is the feeling of emptiness, boredom, and discontentment, bordering on melancholy. It refers to those times when we live in our own little world, are asleep, are unguarded, and try to put our restlessness to death with nervous distractions. Here no therapy can help us but only healing.[5] God's Spirit must come in order to fill us and make us complete. Outside of that movement, we are lost.

We ourselves do not control the coming of the Spirit and his indwelling. It remains a gift, an act of God, who must continue to send his Spirit. In numerous Lord's Days, the catechism mentions the effects of God's Spirit on our lives. In Lord's Day 38, for example, it draws a connection to the day of rest: we must give the Spirit room to go to work.

One modern theologian faced head-on the demon of acedia: Karl Barth. His theology is an extreme example of a reflection in which Christians are reminded time and time again that they should not assume too easily that God is on their side. In the second edition of his Romans commentary Barth formulated the possession of the Spirit in terms of non-identity: the new person is a "non-ego."[6] The theology of the *Church Dogmatics* goes on to specify that God is and remains the subject in all his work. In the doctrine of reconciliation

---

5. Kathleen Norris, *Acedia and Me: A Marriage, Monks, and a Writer's Life* (New York: Riverhead Books, 2008), 141.

6. Karl Barth, *Der Römerbrief (Zweite Fassung) 1922*, ed. Cornelis van der Kooi and Katja Tolstaja (Zürich: Theologischer Verlag, 2010), 398-99.

the new person is Jesus Christ. The newness can be deemed and recounted only as a witness—not of our conversion and experiences but of Jesus Christ.

But does Barth overlook an element of the biblical witness in his theology? It seems so. He is always extremely careful in acknowledging any human contribution, which is at once the power as well as the weakness of his theology. And yet, we cannot escape the biblical texts that do indeed point to a participation on the part of humans that is counted as their own activity.

Paul is not afraid of employing language that describes human activity. He calls upon his addressees to put on the new human being as a coat or a new garment (Eph. 4:20-24). He declares himself to be taking part in a race that is not yet finished (Phil. 3:12-14). Participation in Christ aims at the transformation of the life of the human being (2 Cor. 3:18). The grand narrative of God's turning toward us should be translated into the everyday, personal events, at the individual, familial, and communal levels. The Holy Spirit inserts traces in the life and times of people, of communities, and perhaps also of cultures, as Kuyper, Van Ruler, Berkhof, and Niebuhr have argued. But can it in a culture be more than a trace? A trace is an impression, not the Holy Spirit himself, and always also other spirits, which are not God's Spirit, can appear. Nevertheless, traces of the Holy Spirit can be bedrocks, wadis in the desert, which he can suddenly fill. But now I touch upon something that will be addressed in the last chapter.

Another term for anointing is "baptism with the Spirit." Frank Macchia has suggested that this term ought no longer to be used with its restricted application and should instead be understood as a qualifier for all the Spirit's work in faith, conversion, renewal, witness, and life. This notion obtains its breadth and depth in the appearance of Jesus, since he, led and carried along by the Spirit, revealed the kingdom of God in the full extent of its liberating and healing significance.[7] I would argue that the phrase "baptism with the Spirit" may be used in a broad sense, following the pattern of the way the anointing of Christ has functioned in the Reformed tradition. This usage admittedly involves renewed reflection on two fronts. First, it will be necessary to work out in greater detail what the Reformed tradition has up to the present said about the anointing or baptism with the Spirit. Second, it will be necessary to restore to the phrase "baptize with the Spirit" its broad range of meaning. In the history of Methodism, the Holiness Movements, and Pentecostalism, Spirit baptism has come to be reduced to a "second blessing," but this restriction can only be considered a mistake.

Sharing in His Anointing:
The Royal Rule of Christ through the Spirit

What does it mean that people participate in Jesus's anointing or baptism? The Heidelberg Catechism sets out the threefold office in the order of prophet, priest, king (Lord's Day 12). These three are all dimensions of Christ's one office.

Here I would like to begin with the kingly office. Christ's kingship came first and did not begin at the ascension, as Calvin would have it. Jesus's kingship was a fundamental dimen-

---

7. Frank D. Macchia, *Baptized in the Spirit: A Global Pentecostal Theology* (Grand Rapids: Zondervan, 2006).

sion of his earthly life. Wherever Jesus went, the contours of God's kingdom became visible; the work of the eschatological Spirit was palpable. There liberation of life took place, people were reunited with the God of Israel, and they learned to do justice. There people no longer belonged to themselves or their past, but something more powerful was paving a way for itself and came to overwhelm them. It provided healing—as indicated in the notion of anointing. It became a reality in the life of Christ. As the New Adam, he took up the covenant with God and brought this life with God to fulfillment. His was a new regime that became visible in his appearance; he lived this new regime, and it brought about the beginnings of restoration. It was a regime in which union with the living God was realized.

In his way of acting, Jesus manifested a sort of superiority over against other forms of the exercise of power. Jesus was said to act with authority (*exousia*). He cast out the demons who held people captive and was convinced that in his acts God's reign became realized (Mark 1:21–28). When he was confronted with his earthly judges—with Pilate as representative of the government and with the judges of the Sanhedrin as representatives of the temple and Torah—his words and actions expressed an intriguing autonomy and confidence. He knew of another authority behind him, knowing himself to be the envoy of the highest king, the highest sovereign (Mark 14:62). This testimony of another kingship continued through to his execution. He died on the cross with the inscription "The King of the Jews." This inscription, meant as a mockery, was not without reason interpreted by the ruling Jews as ambivalent and subversive. Therefore they urgently requested Pilate to remove it (John 19:21).

How does the Spirit of the eschaton work on the followers of Christ, on his church? By sharing in a new kingdom in which the powers of the old world no longer have the upper hand, and in which the Spirit of the end times is at work instead. Recognition of Jesus's kingship means first of all that a congregation or church comes into existence whose members *confess that they have passed over from the kingdom of death into the kingdom of life.* It begins with a transition or transfer whose relevance does not pertain just to eternal life but which is in a certain sense already active now. The church clings stubbornly to this story. We are no longer our own, a truth the catechism expresses in terms of belonging. Those who place their hope in Christ no longer belong to the devil and his kingdom, to a social class or ethnic entity, to modern powers like Google or Facebook or the Stock Exchange. Rather, they are Christ's possession. This transition from death to life, this declaration of belonging receives its form and expression in the sign of baptism. Baptism is not, as Barth would have it, a human testimony as the counterpart to a Spirit baptism that has already taken place. Rather, the immersion in water makes one share in a certain way in effecting this transition. What happens physically in the water of baptism, in word and sign, is taken by God into his service. For that reason baptism is not in the first place a family event, nor ought it in any way to be seen as a kind of baby shower. Christian baptism must be torn from the clutches of civil initiation rites and be restored to its dramatic significance.

The ritual of baptism with water unites the human being with the death and resurrection of Christ. It marks the transition from estrangement to the covenant of life. It proclaims publicly that Christ is the legitimate Lord of this human and his or her life. On the human side, a response is made in which the human being as a disciple practices a life in which the powers that estrange us from God no longer dominate. Christian life therefore requires lifelong exercise, meaning that in every phase of life new challenges appear. Childhood, adolescence, adulthood, middle age, and aging adult—they all require response.

A second characteristic that flows from the foregoing is the "eccentric" structure of Christian identity; that is, there is now a new center. Christ is Lord, and the order of his love and grace should reign and nothing else. All leadership and execution of power should be measured by this criterion. A biblical reminder of this criterion appears in Psalm 72 and also in the story of the introduction of kingship in Israel, which is described as a concession to the Israelites. The request to be ruled by a king is received by the prophet Samuel as a rejection of God (1 Sam. 8:4-9). This negative characterization of human kingship forms a critical reminder for all forms of leadership. The desacralization of emperor, king, leader, president, or CEO has deep roots in the confession of the church. The only real king is Jesus of Nazareth, who was crucified in an allied action of politics, law, religion, and people who, in their own eyes, were acting appropriately.

I add a highly significant third element. Participation in this dimension of Christ's anointing implies renewal or transformation. In order to understand this element, we can refer again to the adoption metaphor. As we have already seen, adoption means that someone becomes part of a new family and must try to feel at home in new surroundings with its own rules and ambiance. He or she takes a seat at the table, which may aptly be called a welcome table, and becomes a

Criterion for Living the Christian Life

part of that new environment. Adoption means the arrival of a new constellation, a new order—an order of love and justice. In that family, the most important rule for life, however, is not self-preservation, but precedence is given to the experience of making and giving room. The new family member receives clothing, food, and a place to sleep, all of which bring one in touch with the new experience of grace. Those who have tasted this new life and order have thereby access to a new reign where a "creative, free self-withdrawal on behalf of others" is the new option.[8] This is the order that is operative in the kingdom of God.

This new experience of grace and love at the same time has wider transformative effects on culture and society. Depending on the context, it is reasonable to assume that one's personal life, as well as one's surroundings, culture, and moral order, is influenced by this story. Where the story of the Good Samaritan is told, there a greater receptivity is felt for notions of compassion, consideration, and justice. An "agapic" revolution takes place. "Transforming processes may take place—temporarily and with a certain fragility, indeed—in the fundamental notions according to which a society understands itself."[9]

As the body of Christ, the church or congregation is the place where God receives thanks for this new constellation. Christian worship services are the basic human response to the divine work. This is where salvation is proclaimed and where life is conquered for Christ in worship, proclama-

---

8. See Michael Welker, *God the Revealed: Christology* (Grand Rapids: Eerdmans, 2013), 224-25.

9. G. Buijs, "Tegenwind van Geest," in *De werking van de Heilige Geest in de Europese cultuur en traditie*, ed. E. Borgman et al. (Kampen: Kok, 2008), 35.

tion, testimonies, sacraments, and diaconal service. In the Reformed-Pentecostal dialogue this area was described as one where Reformed and Pentecostals could each learn much from the other.

The Ministry of Healing

I highlight here one element that has come under discussion within evangelical and Reformed spirituality, namely, the ministry of healing, or anointing of the sick. A first thing to say is that, as we engage these questions, we stand on holy ground and should not approach too easily. I consider the anointing of the sick a meaningful act by means of which the church expresses its faith in the life-giving and transforming power of Christ's Spirit. Naturally this practice raises the question of the relationship between prayer and healing. Time and again there are fierce debates in the Netherlands over the phenomenon of healing services and faith healers. How are people and churches to respond? Are all these things to be rejected? We read in the New Testament how Jesus performed healings as a sign of the coming of the kingdom—can such actions now be ignored? Jesus came to earth as a healer. Reports of healing upon or after prayer similarly come to us from the world church. Reformed theology cannot afford simply to shrug off these reports.

In the modernist paradigm in which the churches of the Northern Hemisphere have by now lived for quite some time, miracles or healings are more or less excluded. Cessationism has driven healing back to the time of the early church, which implies a near-complete acceptance of the modern division of life into separate spheres, according to which we have surrendered the sphere of health and illness to the medical sciences. Yet, do the Bible and the experiences of the worldwide church really allow us to do so? And what about Blumhardt, Stanger, the revivals in Wales, Korea, Los Angeles, Toronto, Lourdes? Furthermore—and more important—in the light of the holistic character of the kingdom of God that Jesus brought about, there is much more to say and to do. In this light, it is an altogether positive development that many churches are beginning to devote attention to the anointing of the sick. What the Heidelberg Catechism says about believers' participation in the anointing of Christ suddenly appears to be unused wiring for an actual socket.

Admittedly this line of thought raises a plethora of questions. Does prayer for the sick not quickly run the risk of becoming like magic? And what are we to say about the many cases in which the sick stay sick and pass away? We stand on holy ground.

In this context it is worthwhile referring to three theses from a document drafted in 2007 by the Charismatische Werkgemeenschap Nederland and the Nederlandse Lukas Orde (Netherlands Charismatic Association and Netherlands Order of St. Luke):[10]

> **2.** Part of the commission of the Christian church is to pray for and with people. As human beings, we are exposed to all kinds of misery and dangers, including sit-

---

10. "Gebed en genezing. Gezamenlijke verklaring van de Charismatische Werkgemeenschap Nederland en de Nederlandse Lucasorde," *Geestkracht. Bulletin voor Charismatische Theologie* 79 (2017): 56–57.

uations of illness where people suffer psychological or physical threats. By prayer they are entrusted in their state of brokenness to the life-giving power of God. Following international usage, we refer to this as the "ministry of healing." This ministry is in practice often accompanied by the laying on of hands and/or anointing and has a place alongside other ministries like the ministry of mercy. Healing ministry can be seen as a pastoral ministry. It is a part of the overarching ministry of Word and sacrament. For this reason we recommend the ministry of healing as an essential ministry of the church's life.

3. The ministry of healing does not compete with modern medicine; the two ought instead to be viewed as partners that are together searching for a human existence. The science and practice of medicine provide alleviation and healing. In the ministry of healing the whole person who is looking for deliverance and healing is brought into God's presence. According to that encounter with God they gratefully receive what God wills to give them. We consider modern medicine to be a gift from God. For that reason we fiercely oppose all forms of ministry in which medical interventions are considered inferior to the ministry of healing or other spiritual forms of healing.

4. Prayer for and with the sick in the ministry of healing occurs in a context of expectation and perseverance. Yet this does not mean we are certain that we will receive exactly what we pray for. In prayer and the laying on of hands people entrust themselves to God's protecting and life-giving power. In his compassion God himself is the beginning and the end. How the prayers are heard is up to God alone, who is all-powerful in all his acts, as well as merciful and faithful. On the one hand, this gives us the courage to pray persistently; on the other hand, it means that our expectation of total perfection in the present has its limits. Christ's resurrection does not mean an immediate renewal of man and world. Perfection is yet to come. At the present time the Spirit of God is groaning together with us. The Spirit makes us share in the salvation of Christ in a way that does not undo the reality of our cross and suffering. The Kingdom of God is carving out a path for itself, but it is not yet complete.

These propositions create room for the charismata to play a role. Implicitly they make it clear that there is openness to the gifts of grace, including those of healing, and that prayer for healing is a duty.

It should not be ignored that, at the time and place appointed by him, God sends gifts that help the church in its service to the church and the world. They make us better. But what precisely this "better" is, is determined by God alone.

The Priestly Dimension

The second dimension of the threefold office is priestly. This office makes us think back to the temple service, which was fulfilled in Jesus because he radically engaged himself for the sake of God's kingdom and in the process paid the ultimate sacrifice. It is important here that the sacrificial ministry not be reduced to sin offerings and the burnt offering on the Day of Atonement. Daily sacrifices were brought to the temple, along with thank offerings for a variety of occasions marking the progress of life. The burnt offering and the sin offering served this progress in situations where life had met with serious obstacles. In the New Testament, Jesus appears through the prism of the sacrificial ministry, as being at once priest and sacrifice. The priestly dimension of Jesus comes to expression in his compassion—over those who experience misery, regardless of whether they themselves share in the guilt, have isolated themselves, or have been victimized by oppression or injustice. This message of godly compassion marks a significant difference from the ministry of John the Baptist. His ministry was marked by the preaching of doom, the announcement of judgment, and the plea to repent before it was too late. Jesus announces the "year of the Lord's favor," where the focus is on restoration. On God's behalf, he offers progress and reverses the estrangement.

The actions of Jesus simultaneously show royal and priestly features. But exactly this acting in the name of his Father, together with the claim that in his preaching and acts God himself instigates the final restoration, provokes disapproval and resistance. The leaders of the people neither recognize nor acknowledge in this man the envoy of the God of Israel. By that very response their estrangement from God is manifest. The guilt and estrangement of the spiritual and political leaderships appear in the condemnation and execution of Jesus. But exactly this condemnation by human beings becomes a place and fulcrum for decisive change. God acts decisively in this human act of condemnation, transforming it to his own eschatological verdict against all the estrangement to which the race of Adam has been held captive. The

Criterion for Living the Christian Life

transformation of the cross from a mere catastrophe to a vindication of God's love and a victory over sin and estrangement is the surprising message of the New Testament. The exalted and glorified Lord is pictured with the features of the earthly Jesus. In the Letter to the Hebrews, Jesus is priest in the heavenly sanctuary and intercedes for those who are his. He is lion and lamb at the same time; in this image the royal features go together with the priestly (Rev. 5:5-7).

But how does this priestly regime of Christ manifest itself visibly in our world? The catechism speaks about a "living sacrifice of thankfulness" and a "free conscience." The eccentric structure of the Christian life immediately becomes visible. Our life draws heavily on the reconciliation achieved between God and humanity, which we ourselves do not have to work to achieve. Jesus's life, efforts, and commitment are the gifts that break the powers of death and guilt. At the same time, the Bible also emphasizes human subjectivity. Following Romans 12:1, the catechism speaks about a "living sacrifice of thankfulness." That is, the sacrifice of thankfulness is not something lifeless, but the person is a subject who places his or her life actively and consciously in the service of God's compassion.[11] In this way, Christ as head puts into action the powers in his body, whose members are the believers. The Spirit is the agent of a differentiated convergence of powers and possibilities through which Christ's mercy is given concrete shape in the world. It can be realized in reconciliation between people, colleagues, husbands and wives, and some-

11. Welker notices that the Barmen Declaration places all emphasis upon Christ as Lord, with the activity of the human being remaining underexposed (*God the Revealed*, 237).

times in a process of inner healing. But when it comes so close, we are scared; we're not comfortable when the Healer comes too close. Often we do not want to have the trauma uncovered—like the man at the pool of Bethesda, who had his infirmity for thirty-eight years (John 5:1-15).

The Eucharist, or Lord's Supper, is the place where paradigmatically the unity and effect of Christ and his church is given shape. In 2 Corinthians 5:19-20 Paul speaks about the ministry of reconciliation and entreats his audience to *be* reconciled to God. Those who partake of the Eucharist must admit reconciliation in their lives and leave room for it. They have to be active in this respect. They can also just leave the door closed. In the Eucharistic prayer we find a sobering reminder, and a dark shadow passes in front of us when it refers to the "night on which he was betrayed." Particularly at the table of the Lord's Supper, participants are reminded that the betrayal of Jesus of Nazareth did not come from outside but from within the very circle of his own followers. This is an important, unsettling lesson: among those who know Jesus and what he has done, there may be exasperation and disappointment over the absence of visible results; in the end, some may decide to leave that circle and quit.[12]

A second element of the priestly office is the progress it provides. The temple service was intended to serve the progression of society and human life. That progress pertained both to regular daily life and to situations of guilt and loss.

12. Welker, *God the Revealed*, 298: "Through announcing Christ's death in the celebration of Holy Communion, the congregation . . . renews the consciousness of being part of humankind that repeatedly, and with all possible means, tries to obscure and distort God's presence and the salvation and well-being for the world."

That progression must be given a place in the restricted confines of the family, friends, and neighborhood but should also be translated into the broader sphere of politics and law. Where society is served by politics and government for the sake of the progress of human life and community, where families offer children room and involvement, there something appears of the priestly aspect for which we offer thanks to God.

The Prophetic Dimension

Although in the tradition the prophetic dimension of Christ's singular office comes first, I have chosen to treat it here as the third and final one. What is the prophetic element? The prophetic means that the light is turned on as we clearly see where we stand in the light of God's benevolence. This happens in the context of a good church service, marking the church as a missionary movement—although the latter is not the topic I wish to address at the present time. It is necessary for us also to become familiar with the prophetic as something closer to home.

In the Heidelberg Catechism, we read that Christ as prophet and teacher reveals the counsel of God to us. If we no longer interpret God's counsel as a blueprint but as the revelation of his good will, his benevolence, then we can leave behind the abstract tone of the word "counsel" in Reformed doctrine. God's counsel is in the end nothing else than the living God himself. In Christ and his life, we see the *Deus decernens*, the God who turns himself toward his children and brings about his grace. Christ's acts and speech are the salvific will of God, literally the *euangelion*, or good message. Thus he is the *prophētēs*, literally, the voice of God. The story of Jesus in the synagogue at Nazareth, where he quotes the words of Isaiah 61, is paradigmatic (Luke 4:14-30). He announces that it is the "year of the Lord's favor" (v. 19), the jubilee year, which was to bring restoration for all and the whole society. Jesus thus speaks the truth, God's truth, point blank.

How and where do believers partake in this prophetic office? The Reformation has located the prophetic office in the ministry of the Word, not in the actions of prophetic figures who were said to have a word or vision from the Lord. The work of the Spirit was strictly bound to the given Word, the Scriptures, which were ministered to the people in proclamation. Against this background it is understandable that the weekly Bible expositions, which were a custom in the Swiss Reformation, were named Prophezei, or prophecy.[13]

Karl Barth gave a fruitful reinterpretation to the prophetic dimension when he in *Church Dogmatics* IV/3 developed the notion of witness. He did so in continuity with the trajectory of a distinction that ran like a red thread through his theology, beginning with the second edition of his commentary on Romans, namely, the qualitative difference between God and human beings. Jesus Christ is the one who witnesses to himself. The very most people can do is to assist in this witness to Christ.[14] Christ himself is the actor. The paradox in Barth's reinterpretation of the prophetic office of Christ lies, on the one hand, in his contributing enormously to the

13. Erik de Boer, *The Genevan School of the Prophets: The congrégations of the Company of Pastors and Their Influence in Sixteenth-Century Europe* (Geneva: Librairie Droz, 2012), 32-33.
14. Barth, *Church Dogmatics* IV/3, 602.

understanding that the church is called to mission while, on the other hand, being very careful (perhaps too careful!) to ensure that not too much attention was given to the means of grace (*media gratiae*). Nevertheless, he gave ample attention to the notion of witness. The notions of witness and the church as a witness are entirely in line with deeply biblical notions and take up elements that shaped the faith experience of Methodism and Pentecostalism. Testimonies are not only a well-known genre in the Acts of the Apostles, but we also find them as a fixed element in many free churches and in revival circles. It is further worth noting that, in the present time and context, Stanley Hauerwas has fruitfully developed the notion of witness as an ethical category.

Reformed theology and practice can still learn much about the prophetic office as a means of grace. To prophesy means to declare where we now stand in the light of God's appearance in Christ. In that sense, prophecy occurs in a broader and more diverse set of forms than the ministry of Word and sacraments as means of grace. Above, we noted the diversity and polyphony of the Spirit's work. This polyphony also means that our nonmental capacities may be engaged in order to praise God and to testify to the presence of a new life. Imagination, emotion, creativity, musical talents—the Spirit can use many different means to witness to Christ. In Pentecostal and free churches, there is greater awareness of these avenues of the Spirit of Christ than there has been in the traditional churches. If I am not mistaken, traditional churches currently find themselves in a learning phase. At times it is necessary to learn to look with new eyes at existing practices. I mention two examples.

If prophecy is the announcement of how the world now

looks in the light of God's appearance in Christ, we can already detect much more of prophecy going on in a traditional Presbyterian context than simply sermon and exposition alone. What I refer to here is congregational singing. When the congregation sings psalms and songs, the church takes up its function as "God's own people, in order that you may proclaim the mighty acts of him who called you out of darkness into his marvelous light" (1 Pet. 2:9). When, following a meal, Dutch families used to sing a song together or read a Bible story with the children and the other guests, this is not just a song or a story but proclamation of God's truth. Similarly, prayers before or after the meal form a part of prophetic and priestly activity as well. As faith practices, they might be assessed as possible avenues of the work of the Spirit.

I do not have the space here to enumerate and treat everything that is a part of this prophetic dimension (which certainly includes politics and public life), nor do I want to. Aside from music, it is necessary to mention glossolalia as an opportunity that has been given to God's church and can suddenly manifest itself there. Speaking in tongues is not normative, but it still is something that the church or individuals may receive. It bears pointing out that glossolalia ought not to be confused with ecstasy, in which someone's consciousness is turned off. Rather, speaking in tongues is a form of praise that has no propositional content. Compared to articulated speech, it is a form of abstraction, one that lacks meaning. It serves our concentration on God and the praise of God (cf. 1 Cor. 14:2). Speaking in tongues is a form of prayer and praise whereby a person's heart is with the Lord without clear concepts. It can be compared to a nonfigurative painting: there is no concrete reality, and yet a reality is being

Criterion for Living the Christian Life

mediated. Glossolalia ought further to be distinguished from xenolalia, which is the miracle described to us in Acts 2. In this account, every person heard the apostles speak in their own language.[15] This phenomenon cannot be relegated to the past, and it is in fact easy to explain within a pneumatological and missional context. The Holy Spirit is a bridge builder, the *pontifex maximus*, who brings Christ and his gifts (*charismata*) to each person in his or her specific circumstances. The Spirit is the interpreter who brings Christ's salvation close to us, down to our own language. This is the missiological aspect of the gift of prophecy. It alone is reason enough for theology to have the task of translating the gospel into the vernacular.

In the midst of this diversity, one thing remains clear: if the Spirit takes from what belongs to Christ and gives it to us, various media or avenues may be used to which Protestant theology has given very little, if any, attention—dreams, visions, words of wisdom, words from the Lord; even the architecture of a building and modern media may become an avenue of the work the Spirit of Christ does with us. They can all be considered means of grace.

---

15. Cornelis van der Kooi, *Tegenwoordigheid van Geest* (Kampen: Kok, 2006), 87.

6 Eyes and Ears Open to the World
Discernment and Hope

Signs of the Spirit?

Where is the Spirit moving? Where is the kingdom of God emerging? Can we perceive signs and traces of God's lifegiving Spirit? Or is the world void and the cosmos we inhabit simply a barren wilderness, where chaos and injustice have free play? We can draw the circle tighter and restrict ourselves to the life sphere of our daily work, family, relatives, friends, and our own body, or we can extend it somewhat wider to include our neighborhood, city, or country. Do we find meaning, content, and satisfaction, or is daily reality full of holes, spots where we feel the vanity of it all? In chapter 5, we discussed this question in terms of participation. According to the Christian faith, we benefit from a benevolent force, which in the language of Christian tradition can be identified as the Spirit of Christ. We even specified this participation as "anointing" or "baptism with the Spirit." The concept of anointing points to something overwhelming and absorbing. In contemporary language, we would rather speak of a bath or shower, which might also be associated with wellness,

Discernment and Hope

well-being, and abundance. The New Testament places the power of that benevolent force first of all in Jesus of Nazareth. Subsequently, it tells us that this power was poured out on the disciples and took possession of ordinary men and women. It is the power of love that, according to Paul, has been poured into our hearts through the Holy Spirit (Rom. 5:5). This Spirit is the driving force that bound the apostle to his apostolate. And by the inspiration of God's Spirit, people crossed borders and became the gospel part of the lives of other people and other cultural contexts. The Spirit of Christ sees to it that the reign of Christ is at work in a multiplicity of circumstances, settings, and dimensions. In chapter 5 the dimensions of this anointing were described as the royal, priestly, and prophetic dimensions of Christ's one office. This functional terminology can, however, be translated into more ordinary concepts. The "royal" stands for a way of life where love is formative for communal life; the "priestly" dimension has its focus in restoration, liberation, and mercy; and "prophetic" means that things will come into the light as they really are, that is to say, as they are in God's eyes. In this final chapter, I take up the question of God's presence and activity once again, but this time we will be drawing the circle wider.

How and where does the Spirit work? Psalm 24 declares: "The earth is the LORD's and all that is in it, the world, and those who live in it" (v. 1). The universal range of God's power is also confessed in the New Testament. He is the alpha and the omega; to him has been given all power in heaven and on earth. At the same time, there is still the hiddenness of his reign, rebellion against Christ's lordship, and the "not yet" of God's kingdom. The final and complete revelation and unveiling of Christ's kingship is still a matter of hope and awaits fulfillment (2 Tim. 4:1; Rev. 12:10). In Matthew, the future judge is already present in a hidden way with those who suffer from oppression and sickness, from banishment and imprisonment (Matt. 25:31-46). The Gospel of John provides us with the image of the good shepherd who calls his sheep. They know his voice. Yet, how do we discern the voice of the good shepherd from other voices? This question brings us to a practice that was already part of Jesus's own life and is recounted to us in the narrative of the temptation in the desert. It is a practice that has become known from the writings of the Desert Fathers, namely, discernment (*discretio*), which more generally can be found in the mystical tradition of the Eastern and the Western churches, in Puritan and pietistic circles, in Pentecostalism, and within the churches of the Southern Hemisphere.[1]

Discernment and the Quest for Authority

In Reformed theology, the question of discernment is mainly answered by pointing to the community of the church, the place where the Word is preached and the sacraments are administered. The practice of preaching and of the administration of the sacraments in fact demarcates the space where it is supposed that God speaks. In chapter 4 we discussed the word pair "Word and Spirit." God rules by his Word and Spirit.[2] The importance of this word pair is illustrated by its having even become a part of the idiom of the Dutch rhymed

1. K. Waayman, "Discernment and Biblical Spirituality: An Overview and Evaluation of Recent Research," *Acta Theologica Supplementum* 17 (2013): 1-12.

2. Heidelberg Catechism, questions 21, 31, 54, 123.

Discernment and Hope

version of Psalm 25, second stanza. As we have stated above, Word and Spirit functioned as the demarcation of the way in which God deals with his children. It was used in connection with the Bible as Holy Scripture. For Reformed worship the church buildings may be sober, and at most one may encounter instances of material religion such as an open Bible, the eucharistic cup, and a baptismal font. In the iconography of the Reformation, that sober spirituality has become visible in the wonderful paintings of Rembrandt or of Gerard Dou depicting an old woman reading the Bible. This is the Reformed "saint," a woman in concentration on the Word of God. Such physical elements and pictures make it tangible that, in all the debates surrounding the Bible, it is not so much the authority of the Bible that is at stake but the question of trust. What can I rely on, where does my soul find a safe haven? Reformed theology, or more precisely, Reformed spirituality, answered the question of spiritual formation with the two words "Word" and "Spirit." Word is the physical Bible and the audible proclamation of God's promises; the Holy Spirit is the inner coach. What is significant is the frequently affective language that is used for that inner coach who is at work. The Holy Spirit does not skim over the life of the children of God, but he forms it and molds their heart and will.[3]

The Word is the proclaimed Word, which is more than a one-sided address. It is *discourse*, in which the discourse partner is called upon. This understanding once more points to the space of the congregation, the faith community, and

3. C. van der Kooi, "De Heilige Geest volgens de Heidelberger Catechismus," in *Handboek Heidelberger Catechismus*, ed. Arnold Huijgen et al. (Utrecht: Kok, 2013), 240–41, 247.

the ministry of the Word. In that space, one learns to discern the voice of the Good Shepherd as the voice that addresses everyone personally. Following Calvin's idiom, a specific term came to be coined for that inner process of persuasion: the inner testimony of the Holy Spirit (*testimonium internum Spiritus Sancti*). This inner testimony is the work of the Spirit that gives us assurance about the promise of God.

With this explicit bond between Spirit and Word, the Reformation directly countered the notion that the Spirit gives new revelations. It thus attacked the spiritualist movement, which appealed to the freedom of God's Spirit and to the inner Word over against the dead letter of the Bible. On the other side, the Reformers resisted the view of the Roman Catholic Church, which bound the Spirit primarily to the church. This debate with the Roman Catholic position is displayed paradigmatically in the epistolary exchange between Cardinal Jacopo Sadoleto and John Calvin. Sadoleto had warned the citizens of Geneva that, in order to be assured of eternal life and salvation, they ought to stay under the custody of the church, since the Holy Spirit has bound himself to it. Calvin responded that God has bound the Spirit not to the church but to his Word. With that response, Bible and proclamation were placed on the center of the stage.

Even today, Sadoleto's response is as simple as it is intriguing. Who, in the final analysis, is the person or authority who has to explain the Word? Where does the discernment of the Spirit find its place? Does the Protestant world not find itself in great embarrassment when history shows there have been a multitude of mutually conflicting Bible expositors who all claim to have the right explanation? Who is the referee in all of this, or is there just a disturbingly great multitude of authorities? Not only is the existence of the magisterium very practical, but there is also ample biblical basis for the close relationship between the Spirit and the apostles. Or should we rather assess the question of Word and Spirit differently? Does the Reformation position not testify of greater trust, patience, and awareness of the polyphony of the Spirit insofar as it does not locate the Holy Spirit exclusively with the Roman bishop's magisterial office? I think here of the question with which Karl Barth staggered his hosts on his visit to the Second Vatican Council. In a meeting with other prelates, Joseph Ratzinger spoke extensively on the church and could mention wonderful things. Eberhard Busch reports Barth's reaction: "We Protestants stand completely poor alongside this wealth. But why did you until now not speak, at least not explicitly, on the Holy Spirit? And for what reason does tradition play such a dominating role for the Roman Catholic Church? Does this somehow stem from fear of the Holy Spirit? My dear Herr Ratzinger, might it be that your church in fact is on the run from the Holy Spirit?"[4]

Here I do not wish to discuss whether it is fruitful to contrast the relationship between Spirit and church so sharply with what in Reformed theology is discussed as the relationship between Spirit and Word. Instead, I want to ask what means have been given to us to perceive the work of the Holy Spirit in the world. What are the places or instances where we can speak of anointing with the Spirit? By what criteria can the voice of the Good Shepherd be recognized?

---

4. E. Busch, *Meine Zeit mit Karl Barth* (Göttingen: Vandenhoeck & Ruprecht, 2011), 230.

Discernment in Recent Dialogue

One of the areas where Reformed and Pentecostal theology will have to engage in a continuing exchange of ideas and in dialogue is the question of the discernment of the spirits. I consciously use the plural form here, although in essence there is no difference between "discernment of the Spirit" and "discernment of the spirits." Both phrases refer to the recognition of God's voice, the guidance of his Spirit. In the most recent dialogue between representatives from the World Alliance of Reformed Churches and several classic Pentecostal churches (in which I was honored to participate), agreement could be reached on numerous issues—with the exception of this very point. In that line, it is very telling that the notion of the discernment of the spirits does not occur in traditional Reformed theology. This is not to suggest that Reformed theology has no interest in how the faith community can learn to discover the voice of the Good Shepherd; rather, it formulates that question using the terms we discussed above, namely, Word and Spirit. With this, Reformed theology emphasizes the normative status of the Bible as the Word of God vis-à-vis current-day experiences. It formulates the active guidance of God christologically. To quote the words of Lord's Day 12 in the Heidelberg Catechism, Christ is "our eternal King, who governs us by His Word and Spirit, and who defends and preserves us in the redemption obtained for us." The exalted Lord is the acting subject of that guidance, and as the Head of his body (i.e., the church), he is dynamically active to defend and preserve it, using the Word and Spirit as his means. What should strike us in this formulation is the dynamic nature of Christ's activity, as well as its continuous nature. Christ is

Discernment and Hope

not passive in heaven, but he works and cares for us through his Spirit.

The necessity of discerning God's will and the search for this will is not an element foreign to the Reformed tradition. The last century in particular has delivered striking examples of moments at which the church felt the call to discern the spirits. I think of the Barmen Declaration (1934), for example, which posits forcefully in thesis 1 that the church must listen to Christ as the one Word of God. And it is to do so against any other powers and institutions that present themselves with divine pretentions or authority. Later, Karl Barth described the declaration as a moment at which the church acted prophetically.[5] We might also mention the Belhar Confession (1986), in which racial segregation is condemned as a heresy. The aforementioned report of the Reformed-Pentecostal dialogue recalls several instances from recent Pentecostal history when the community felt the call to discern God's will more closely, in such matters as the ordination of women to the office of pastor. Appealing to the fact that the Spirit, according to Acts 2:17-18, was poured out on all flesh and that the Spirit out of his sovereignty gave his gifts to those to whom it pleased him to give them, the conclusion was reached in a process of prayer, communal deliberation, and new insight that it was the will of God that women and men share equally

---

5. Barth, *Church Dogmatics* II/1, 176: "The Word of God still remained, in spite of everything, in the same Church in which it had been so often denied and betrayed. . . . That this could be the case certainly has its spiritual-historical, theological and political presuppositions and determinations. But all the same it was impossible, and in the end a miracle, in the eyes of those who saw it at close quarters. And so the first article of Barmen was not merely a pretty little discovery of the theologians."

in the ministerial office from that point. I further note that Kuyper, under the influence of Schleiermacher, drew this same conclusion in 1861.

The Reformed-Pentecostal dialogue also drew a wider conclusion, however, in which other means of revelation were mentioned, aside from the Bible and sermons alone. The report mentions also dreams, visions, revelations, and intuitions as possible means the Holy Spirit may use. In paragraph 101 we read:

> We agree that God continues to speak today through the Word and through the Holy Spirit. This means that God speaks through the narrative of the Bible, and God employs other means as well. We agree that it is important for the church to recognize God's voice wherever it is spoken and to distinguish between the means by which God speaks and the norms of God's revelation. In a fragmented world, and too often fragmented church, there is a critical need for shared discernment of the shape of Christian faith and life.[6]

This passage reflects the ongoing rapprochement between Pentecostals, charismatics, and Reformed, as well as the need for renewed reflection on pneumatology. In Pentecostal circles, charismatic and evangelical groups, and mainline churches in the Southern Hemisphere, we encounter experiences of personal prophecy.[7] That is to say,

---

6. *Reformed World* 63, no. 1 (March 2013): 25.
7. E.g., Cephas N. Omenyo, *Pentecost outside Pentecostalism* (Zoetermeer: Boekencentrum, 2002), 215.

Discernment and Hope

someone receives a word from the Lord, a vision, a dream, or a strong intuition concerning the course the community ought to take or a challenge it is called to assume. And what are we to say about the phenomena of the Toronto Blessing or of the prayer ministry of the New Wine community, each built on the presupposition that God will speak to a group of people who in prayer open themselves to this possibility? How do we know whether it is God who is speaking in these events and phenomena? And what about the channeling and transmissions witnessed in esoteric circles? History presents us with a long line of seers, mystics, and esoterics who claimed to communicate messages to us from a divine, higher world. Think only of Jacob Böhme, Jacob Lorber, Emanuel Swedenborg, Rudolf Steiner, and many others. There are various examples from the church worldwide, in both the Northern and the Southern Hemispheres, of figures who present themselves as prophets and who recognize themselves and/or are recognized by the people around them as mouthpieces of God. What value do their voices have? Can Christian theology help us to be discerning? How are we to deal with this? When do other spirits speak that are not from the Good Shepherd? All these questions are related to the main question of the *discretio animarum*, the discernment of the spirits.

Academic theology has shown itself to be obviously resistant or at least remarkably quiet on this front. Over the last two hundred years, science has experienced ongoing professionalization. In other words, scholarship has sought rational explanation and technical command. In the course of the nineteenth century, this goal led to the distinction between science and pseudoscience (Max Weber and Sigmund Freud).

Accordingly, the medical sciences began to rid themselves of quackery, psychology did away with occultism, and academic theology in the nineteenth century eliminated the themes of revelations and prophecies. From then on, academic theology spoke only of "revelation" in the singular; Jesus Christ is the *one* revelation of God. Theology hardly deals with what the book of Acts reports, namely, that God speaks to people and makes known his will to them. The resistance against charismatic phenomena like prophecies, words from the Lord, or healings is largely dominated by the question of worldview, or what Charles Taylor has called "social imaginary." Western culture, with its emphasis on rational control and immanent explanation, has the tendency to reduce all prophecy, visions, and gifts of healing and tongues to mental, anthropological, and psychological factors. In line with this reduction, most studies on the spirit world come from the world of anthropology;[8] academic theology has kept itself aloof. In the Southern Hemisphere, in contrast, the recognition of a spirit world plays an important role. There evil spirits are understood to be capable of possessing individuals or even entire communities. As such, the spirituality we encounter there and in certain Pentecostal circles is closer to the Aramaic world in which Jesus himself lived than it is to our modern Western world.[9]

---

8. Waayman, "Discernment and Biblical Spirituality," 5–6.

9. Bas van Os, *Psychological Analyses and the Historical Jesus* (London: T&T Clark, 2011), 155–56. On page 156 Van Os quotes Scurlock and Anderson: "All this may sound very strange to modern ears, but the fact is that attributing diseases to spirits is considerably closer to the modern theory of infection by organisms invisible to the naked eye attacking the body from without than is the Hippocratic notion of imbalance of humors."

Criteria for Recognizing God's Spirit in Prophetic Phenomena

Irrespective of the particular worldview that may underlie a prophetic, charismatic, or esoteric manifestation, and regardless of how strange the form of revelation might be, theologically these points are not determinative. Fear is a poor counselor, and the warnings once sounded by Jonathan Edwards are still relevant today.[10] Theologically, what is determinative is what is being said about God and his kingdom. The normative function of systematic theology takes center stage here. The subject who carries out the testing is not the individual but the community. The community, moreover, carries out the testing not arbitrarily but according to several criteria.

1. *Agreement with the Apostles' Creed.* In chapter 5 we used Christ's threefold office as criterion for the church. The manifestations of God's Spirit at the very least must be in line with the elements and narrative that is told in the articles of the Apostolic Creed. This Creed is a rule of faith, a *regula fidei*, that briefly mentions the initiatives and decisive steps that the triune God has made in history. The Apostolic Creed can be regarded as a short summary of salvation history, of the deeds of God, and what on that basis the church believes is yet to come. Within this context, the concept of the threefold office summarizes and comprises the work of Christ. This concept therefore exercises a critical function for all the phenomena

10. Jonathan Edwards, "The Distinguishing Marks of a Work of the Spirit of God," in *The Works of Jonathan Edwards* (Carlisle, PA: The Banner of Truth Trust, 2005), 2:261–66, and also part II of "The Religious Affections" (1746), in *The Works of Jonathan Edwards*, 1:245–62.

and prophecies. For example, where the remembrance of the crucified Christ is denied or reduced to a general identifying badge, there it is a matter of false prophecy.

2. *Recognition of the distinction between God's Spirit and the human spirit.* One of the fundamentals of the Christian faith is that human beings are creatures and, as such, are fundamentally distinct from God. Our human spirit is not identical to God's Spirit. This basic distinction is no plea for a distant God, for God comes near to the human race. Yet, the notion of closeness respects the Creator-creature distinction, even while it also binds them together. Even when the Bible speaks about the indwelling of God's Spirit, this is no declaration of identity. The Spirit of God never becomes a human possession. Negatively, this means that when a word or prophecy announces, for example, a God-man symbiosis or undoes their "otherness," some other spirit is presenting the word. In his closeness, God's otherness benefits us.

3. *The Spirit of God does not point to himself but to Christ.* In the Spirit's work, it is Christ himself who draws near to us. Wherever acts of love and compassion occur, wherever people are placed in the light of the life-giving truth, wherever the new regime of God's kingdom shakes up the social structure and God's creatures are dealt with justly, there Christ is not far away. The Spirit does not claim attention for himself, for his own manifestations, but points away from himself and connects people to Christ. This is a material criterion. In contrast to the Aristotelian or Hegelian concept of spirit, the Holy Spirit is not self-involved, nor is he out to make himself important. In his eccentric structure, he seeks to grant access to the compassion and justice of God, to his will to make people flourish as God's sons and daughters. The Spirit of Christ

Discernment and Hope

is marked by "free self-withdrawal" (Welker), which is how the Spirit breathes new life into a person. He frees one from alien bonds and teaches him or her to walk in this newfound freedom.

4. *The place of good and evil.* The distinction between God and humanity implies the possibility of doing good and evil. For a person to do evil means turning one's back against one's source, while "good" and "fruitful" means that one lives with one's face directed to that source. If prophetic transmissions present evil as a matter of indifference, as a phase in our upbringing, or as a means to grow to greater light, it means that evil is being downplayed. I do not mean that God cannot use illness or suffering as a way to interact with his children, but if we give sin, error, and evil a place of their own in God and so excuse it, this is something altogether different.

5. *From baptism to consummation.* When believers seek baptism, they witness that they want to be connected to Jesus's passage through death. We confess of Christ that death no longer has dominion over him; he has been raised in the eschaton. That is, every prophecy or transmission that claims that after our death we will once more come into this life and under the same conditions is not coherent with the linear nature of the history of Israel and Jesus Christ. It further implies that a triumphalist theology that claims prophetically that we now already fully live under the conditions of consummation and flourishing fails to take account of the fulfillment that still awaits.

6. *The factor of time.* What about prophecy as a personal message, direction, or prediction? What are we to do with these things? According to Deuteronomy 18:22, the criterion for true prophecy is its fulfillment. The same criterion ap-

pears in Jeremiah 28 in connection with the prophet Hananiah, and in Acts 11:28 in the context of Agabus's prophecy regarding a coming famine. In other words, these passages speak about a contemporary speaking of God concerning future events. A faith community must take into account the possibility of such utterances. The criterion of the fulfillment of a prediction focuses our attention on another aspect, namely, the factor of time. It takes time to discover God's will. The counsel of Gamaliel still applies: "If this plan or this undertaking is of human origin, it will fail; but if it is of God, you will not be able to overthrow them—in that case you may even be found fighting against God!" (Acts 5:38-39).

7. *Mutual consultation and prayer.* The fact that discernment of the spirits often has the character of a quest in which we listen to Scripture and to each other has a direct impact on the way in which the church must deal with the ethical questions that deeply divide it worldwide. Testing takes place in the context of the community; it is a matter of the church and of dialogue between the faith communities. As an example, we can think of the deep divisions in the church over same-sex relationships. In this issue the church is confronted with questions concerning relationships, blessing, fertility, and the way men and women relate to each other. Or else consider the questions involving the beginning and end of life. Even more pressing are the questions of injustice, poverty, and exploitation. The salt of the church will have lost its taste if it does not give those questions priority on its agenda. Only if we are prepared to embark upon a process of mutual consultation, prayer, and openness to different kinds of experience may we expect the Spirit to help us.

The Liberating Spirit of Christ in the Modern World

Up to now, I have tried to deal with the question of discernment primarily in terms of the testing of free prophecy, of voices that claim to speak on God's behalf. Existentially there is also another important question related to discernment, namely, the question of where God's redemption manifests itself. This is the question that once was discussed under the rubric of general revelation, that Kuyper addressed in his doctrine of common grace, and that I now want to deal with in terms of God's universality. If the world belongs to God, if the Spirit of Christ is at work, can we then observe the signs of his presence also elsewhere—in politics, culture, media, business and economy, sports, and other religions? How does Christ manifest himself there? Here I wish to use a phrase from the Psalms that was one of Karl Barth's favorites: "In your light we see light" (Ps. 36:9b). In this world, in which powers and forces move about cut off from their source, the Creator, what can we identify as the work of God's Spirit once we have come to know Jesus Christ as the light of the world? Or is this question answered in the response Jesus sent to John when John had asked, "Are you the one who is to come, or are we to wait for another?" (Matt. 11:3).

The ideas already mentioned as part of the threefold office serve as a means to determine what we appreciate as the work of Christ's Spirit in the midst of injustice, estrangement, and open hostility against God. We are more than mere spectators in this drama. In the previous chapter, we mentioned the notion of acedia. We ourselves are the field—the battlefield even—where the struggle takes place in a great melting pot of restlessness, listlessness, and emptiness. The three dimensions of the kingly, the priestly, and the prophetic can help us to decide on our course, to enter society with open eyes and open ears, to dare to take on life, to exercise patience toward others and ourselves, and to be thankful for what is commendable, excellent, and worthy of praise (see Phil. 4:8). We need to emphasize here that this is not about the final consummation, the moment at which Christ's kingship will be revealed to all creation and every knee will bow down before him. Yet, in the meantime we should also gratefully identify certain moments and situations as signs of the coming kingdom.

My expectations, I add, are not for a synthesis of Christianity and culture as it was defended in the High Middle Ages; in nineteenth-century Calvinism; in nineteenth-century Germany by Schleiermacher, Hegel, and Richard Rothe; in the Netherlands by Scholten, Kuyper, Van Ruler, and Berkhof; and in the United States by the brothers Niebuhr and, to some extent still today, in Tim Keller. I also do not plead for a separation between Christian faith and culture, of which the most important proponent was Karl Barth in his Romans commentary and more recently affirmed by John Howard Yoder and Stanley Hauerwas. My plea is for a third way, the way of critical discernment.

Discernment and Hope

Can we imagine for ourselves what the kingdom is like when it appears? Do we theologically have the courage to keep our eyes wide open? In this context Welker has applied the concept of emergence. This term means that, out of a variety of

Discernment and Hope

individual events and elements, a new situation becomes created, an altogether new whole that influences the existence of the individual parts. Here we might think of the dialectics described by Schleiermacher between individual and community. The individual members of the community contribute to the whole so that the whole is then transformed so as to influence the individual parts. Welker points to Jesus's parables of the mustard seed and the sower, where the point of the comparison appears to be the total unexpectedness of a qualitative transformation. In these parables the call to expectation and faith is determinative. The same call is evident in Jesus's response to John the Baptist when the latter was in prison and instructed his disciples to ask Jesus whether Jesus was truly the expected Messiah. It is the dramatic question from someone who had begun to doubt his own expectation as one of Israel's prophets! Jesus's response is as momentous as it is vulnerable and fear-instilling: "Go and tell John what you hear and see: the blind receive their sight, the lame walk, the lepers are cleansed, the deaf hear, the dead are raised, and the poor have good news brought to them" (Matt. 11:4-5). What for John must have been so distressing about Jesus's quotation from Isaiah 61 is that Jesus omits the very thing that pertained most closely to John, namely, the release of prisoners. It amounts to a call to be ready to see the coming of the kingdom in moments of liberation, healing, compassion, and hope, even when immediate and personal fulfillment is absent.

In the New Testament epistles, the transforming work of the Spirit is concentrated on the life of the community and its members. Little attention is devoted to a wider group beyond the immediate, small circle of Jesus's own. The identity of the church is located in that it is "in Christ," and this qualifier produces a large number of imperatives and exhortations. Yet, these very instructions and exhortations have in history had a transforming effect over a wider field. Social institutions for health care, political institutions, the awareness of the equal worth of each and every human being, the care for education—all these things are not a direct result of the "agapic" revolution, but they still are intrinsically bound to it. With his message of neighbor love, including love for one's enemy, Jesus of Nazareth made his contribution to the old world system, or rather he planted a seed that has borne fruit in many and unexpected ways. Warfield, Kuyper, and Bavinck explicitly appreciated the cultural transformations that took place under the yeast of the gospel. The gospel is a "benevolent force" that has come to expression in patterns of care, shared responsibility, and mutual solidarity. Why, then, once the Christian church has discovered Christ as the light of the world, should it not be grateful for all these non-self-evident patterns and institutions, and not discover in this humanity the *humanitas* of Christ and give thanks for it? In your light, we see light.

The Touch of the Spirit

I would like to go back one more time to the film *American Beauty*. A remarkable transition takes place in one scene in this film. Lester, the main protagonist, is long fascinated by his young neighbor Angela. He becomes totally enthralled by this vixen until he discovers a sea of insecurity beneath her mask. For him that moment becomes the discovery of

Discernment and Hope

another role, that of a caring adult. He is able to view himself from a distance, to be liberated from himself, and to do what he has to do, namely, to offer her safety and to leave her untouched. His is a transformation. The film ends with a scene in which Lester is shot dead from behind by his neighbor, a retired US Marine who cannot control his frustrated homosexuality. The spirit of frustration and emptiness seems to dominate; loss and evil are overwhelming. But the smile on the face of the victim witnesses peace, traces of joy. What is the secret of this transformation? Is it the Spirit of Christ who has set him free?

The final step cannot be to recognize theologically that Christ through his Spirit can work also outside the walls of the church (*extra muros ecclesiae*). We should not stop there. It is in no way a plea for the anonymous Christendom promoted by Karl Rahner. The recognition and acknowledgment of the work of the Spirit demand that action be taken. The Spirit points to Christ and to the communion of Father and Son, as we noted. It must be rooted somewhere lest it remain hanging in the air as some sentiment or invention of our own. The phrase "anonymous Christendom" is therefore also a contradiction in terms. Where the Spirit of the Son of the Father is, there the Spirit looks for the recognition of the work of the Son and of the love of the Father. The work of the Spirit as an incredibly benevolent force seeks to be released from anonymity and to work to the honor and praise of the triune God. For that reason we need a church, need faith communities, to practice that praise and to bring us into the realm where evil forces flee. Along the way, and until that is achieved, we are thankful for each and every moment in which God's benevolent power announces itself and touches our reality.

Bibliography

Adam, Alfred. *Lehrbuch der Dogmengeschichte.* Vol. 1. Gütersloh: Mohn, 1970.
Barth, Karl. *Christengemeinde und Bürgergemeinde.* Stuttgart: Kohlhammer, 1946.
———. *Church Dogmatics.* Translated by G. W. Bromiley and T. F. Torrance. 14 vols. Edinburgh: T&T Clark, 1936-75.
———. "Die dogmatische Prinzipienlehre bei Wilhelm Herrmann" (1925). In *Vorträge und kleinere Arbeiten, 1922-1925*, edited by H. Finze, 545-603. Zürich: TVZ, 1990.
———. *Der Römerbrief (Zweite Fassung) 1922*, edited by Cornelis van der Kooi and Katja Tolstaja. Zürich: Theologischer Verlag, 2010.
Bauckham, Richard. *Jesus and the Eyewitnesses: The Gospels as Eyewitness Testimony.* Grand Rapids: Eerdmans, 2006.
Bavinck, Herman. *God and Creation.* Vol. 2 of *Reformed Dogmatics.* Translated by John Vriend. Grand Rapids: Baker Academic, 2004.
Berkhof, Hendrikus. *The Doctrine of the Holy Spirit.* 2nd ed. Richmond, VA: John Knox, 1967.
Boer, Erik de. *The Genevan School of the Prophets: The congrégations of the Company of Pastors and Their Influence in Sixteenth-Century Europe.* Geneva: Librairie Droz, 2012.
Bosch-Heij, Debora van den. *Spirit and Healing in Africa: A Reformed Pneumatological Perspective.* Bloemfontein: Sun Media, 2012.
Bratt, James. *Abraham Kuyper: A Centennial Reader.* Grand Rapids: Eerdmans, 1998.

Buijs, Govert. "Tegenwind van Geest." In *De werking van de Heilige Geest in de Europese cultuur en traditie*, edited by E. Borgman et al., 21-43. Kampen: Kok, 2008.

Busch, Eberhard. *Meine Zeit mit Karl Barth*. Göttingen: Vandenhoeck & Ruprecht, 2011.

Charismatische Werkgemeenschap Nederland. "Gebed en genezing. Gezamenlijke verklaring van de Charismatische Werkgemeenschap Nederland en de Nederlandse Lucasorde." *Geestkracht. Bulletin voor Charismatische Theologie* 79 (2017): 56-57.

Coffey, David. *Deus Trinitas: The Doctrine of the Triune God*. New York: Oxford University Press, 1999.

———. "The Theandric Nature of Christ." *TS* 60 (1999): 405-31.

Diederich, Martin. *Schleiermachers Geistverständnis: Eine systematisch-theologische Untersuchung seiner philosophischen und theologischen Rede von Gott*. Göttingen: Vandenhoeck & Ruprecht, 1999.

Dingemans, Gijsbert J. D. *Het menselijk gezicht van God: Jezus als de unieke drager van de Geest*. Kampen: Kok, 2003.

Dunn, James D. G. *Christology in the Making: A New Testament Inquiry into the Origins of the Doctrine of the Incarnation*. 2nd ed. London: SCM, 1989.

———. *Jesus and the Spirit: A Study of the Religious and Charismatic Experiences of Jesus and the First Christians as Reflected in the New Testament*. London: SCM, 1975.

Edwards, Jonathan. *The Works of Jonathan Edwards*. 2 vols. Carlisle, PA: The Banner of the Truth Trust, 2005.

Fee, Gordon D. *God's Empowering Presence: The Holy Spirit in the Letters of Paul*. 5th printing. Peabody MA: Hendrickson Publishers, 2002.

Feldmeier, Reinhard, and Herrmann Spieckermann. *Der Gott der Lebendigen: Eine biblische Gotteslehre*. Tubingen: Mohr Siebeck, 2011.

Gaventa, Beverly Roberts, and Richard B. Hays, eds. *Seeking the Identity of Jesus: A Pilgrimage*. Grand Rapids: Eerdmans, 2008.

Habets, Mike. *The Anointed Son: A Trinitarian Spirit Christology*. Eugene, OR: Pickwick Publications, 2010.

———, ed. *Third Article Theology: A Pneumatological Dogmatics*. Minneapolis: Fortress, 2016.

Haight, Roger. *Jesus, Symbol of God*. Maryknoll, NY: Orbis, 1999.

Hector, Kevin W. "Actualism and Incarnation: The High Christology

of Friedrich Schleiermacher." *International Journal for Systematic Theology* 8 (2006): 307-22.
Heppe, H., and E. Bizer. *Die Dogmatik der evangelisch-reformierten Kirche*. Neukirchen: Neukirchener Verlag, 1958.
Hesselink, I. John. "Governed and Guided by the Spirit: A Key Issue in Calvin's Doctrine of the Holy Spirit." In *Reformiertes Erbe: Festschrift für Gottfried W. Locher*, vol. 2, edited by H. A. Oberman, 161-71. Zürich: Theologischer Verlag, 1993.
Hick, John. *The Metaphor of God Incarnate: Christology in a Pluralistic Age*. 2nd ed. Louisville: Westminster John Knox, 2005.
Hollenweger, Walter J. *Pentecostalism: Origins and Developments Worldwide*. Peabody, MA: Hendrickson, 1997.
―――. *The Pentecostals*. London: SCM, 1972.
Hurtado, Larry W. *Lord Jesus Christ: Devotion to Jesus in Earliest Christianity*. Grand Rapids: Eerdmans, 2003.
Jenson, Robert W. *Systematic Theology*. Vol. 1. Oxford: Oxford University Press, 1997.
Johnston, Robert K. *Useless Beauty: Ecclesiastes through the Lens of Contemporary Film*. Grand Rapids: Baker Academic, 2004.
Kalsky, Manuela. *Christaphanien: Die Revision der Christologie aus der Sicht von Frauen in unterschiedlichen Kulturen*. Güterlsoh: Gütersloher Verlagshaus, 2000.
Kamp, Gerrit C. van de. *Pneuma-christologie: Een oud antwoord op een actuele vraag?* Amsterdam: Rodopi, 1983.
Kamphuis, B. *Boven en beneden: Het uitgangspunt van de christologie en de problematiek van de openbaring nagegaan aan de hand van de ontwikkelingen bij Karl Barth, Dietrich Bonhoeffer en Wolfhart Pannenberg*. Kampen: Kok, 1999.
Kooi, Cornelis van der. *As in a Mirror: John Calvin and Karl Barth on Knowing God; A Diptych*. Leiden: Brill, 2005.
―――. "De Heilige Geest volgens de Heidelberger Catechismus." In *Handboek Heidelberger Catechismus*, ed. A. Huijgen, John V. Fesko, and Aleide Siller (Utrecht: Kok, 2013), 239-48.
―――. "The Identity of Israel's God: The Potential of the So-Called Extra-Calvinisticum." In *Tradition and Innovation in Biblical Interpretation: Studies Presented to Professor Eep Talstra on the Occasion of His Sixty-Fifth Birthday*, edited by W. T. van Peursen and J. W. Dyk, 209-22. Leiden: Brill, 2011.

---. "Kirche als Lesegemeinschaft: Schrifthermeneutik und Kanon." *VF* 51 (2006): 63-79.

Kooi, Cornelis van der, and Gijsbert van den Brink. *Christian Dogmatics: An Introduction*. Grand Rapids: Eerdmans, 2017.

Krusche, Werner. *Das Wirken des Heiligen Geistes nach Calvin*. Göttingen: Vandenhoeck & Ruprecht, 1957.

Kuyper, Abraham. *Commentatio* (1860). In *Abraham Kuyper's Commentatio (1860): The Young Kuyper about Calvin, a Lasco, and the Church*, vol. 2: *Commentatio*, edited by Jasper Vree and Johan Zwaan. Leiden: Brill, 2005.

---. *The Work of the Holy Spirit* (1910). Grand Rapids: Eerdmans, 1975. Originally in Dutch: *Het werk van de Heilige Geest* (1888). Kampen: Kok, 1927.

Lampe, Geoffrey W. H. *God as Spirit: The Bampton Lectures, 1976*. Oxford: Oxford University Press, 1977.

Lens, Patrick. "God heeft zich aan onze menselijkheid gewaagd." *Comm* 21 (1996): 366-92.

---. "Op Hem bleef de Geest rusten." *Comm* 30 (2005): 9-26.

---. "Schoonenberg en de uniciteit van Christus." In *Verleden openen naar heden en toekomst: Meedenken met de christologie van Piet Schoonenberg*, edited by T. Merrigan and K. Struys, 81-98. Averbode: Altiora, 2001.

Macchia, Frank D. *Baptized in the Spirit: A Global Pentecostal Theology*. Grand Rapids: Zondervan, 2006.

Marthaler, Berard L. *The Creed: The Apostolic Faith in Contemporary Theology*. Mystic, CT: Twenty-Third Publications, 1987.

McCormack, Bruce L. "Über Barth hinaus—mit Schleiermacher?" In *Karl Barth und Friedrich Schleiermacher: Zur Neubestimmung ihres Verhältnisses*, edited by M. Gockel and M. Leiner, 45-88. Göttingen: Vandenhoeck & Ruprecht, 2015.

Nevin, John W. *Mystical Presence: A Vindication of the Reformed or Calvinistic Doctrine of the Eucharist*. Philadelphia: Fisher, 1846.

Norris, Kathleen. *Acedia and Me: A Marriage, Monks, and a Writer's Life*. New York: Riverhead Books, 2008.

Oberman, H. A. "Die 'Extra'-Dimension in der Theologie Calvins." In *Die Reformation: Von Wittenberg nach Genf*, 253-82. Göttingen: Vandenhoeck & Ruprecht, 1986.

Omenyo, Cephas N. *Pentecost outside Pentecostalism: A Study of the*

Development of Charismatic Renewal in the Mainline Churches in Ghana. Zoetermeer: Boekencentrum, 2002.

Os, Bas van. *Psychological Analyses and the Historical Jesus: New Ways to Explore Christian Origins.* London: T&T Clark, 2011.

Pannenberg, Wolfhart. *Systematic Theology.* Vol. 2. Edinburgh: T&T Clark, 1984.

Pelikan, Jaroslav. *The Emergence of the Catholic Tradition (100-600).* Vol. 1 of *The Christian Tradition: A History of the Development of Doctrine.* Chicago: University of Chicago Press, 1971.

Rahner, Karl. *Grundkurs des Glaubens: Einführung in den Begriff des Christentums.* Freiburg: Herder, 1976.

Report of the Reformed-Pentecostal Dialogue. "Experience in Christian Faith and Life: Worship, Discipleship, Discernment, Community, and Justice." *Reformed World* 63, no. 1 (March 2013): 2-44.

Robeck, Cecil M., Jr. *The Azusa Street Mission and Revival: The Birth of the Global Pentecostal Movement.* Nashville: Nelson Reference & Electronic, 2006.

Ruler, A. A. van. *Calvinist Trinitarianism and Theocentric Politics: Essays toward a Public Theology.* Translated and edited by John Bolt. Lewiston, NY: Edwin Mellen, 1989.

Sauter, Gerhard. *In der Freiheit des Geistes.* Göttingen: Vandenhoeck & Ruprecht, 1987.

———. "'Schrifttreue' ist kein 'Schriftprinzip.'" In *Offenbarung und Geschichten*, edited by John Barton and Gerhard Sauter, 21-49. Frankfurt: Peter Lang, 2000.

Schlatter, Adolf. *Das christliche Dogma.* Stuttgart: Calwer, 1923.

Schleiermacher, Friedrich. *Christian Faith* (1830-31). Translated by Terrence N. Tice, Catherine L. Kelsey, and Edwina Lawler. 2 vols. Louisville: Westminster John Knox, 2016.

———. "Die Weihnachtsfeier: Ein Gespräch" (1806). In *Schriften aus der Hallenser Zeit, 1804-1807*, edited by Hermann Patsch, 39-98. Vol. 1.5 of Kritische Gesamtausgabe. Berlin: de Gruyter, 1995.

Schlenke, Dorothee. *Geist und Gemeinschaft: Die systematische Bedeutung der Pneumatologie für Friedrich Schleiermachers Theorie der christlichen Frömmigkeit.* Berlin: de Gruyter, 1999.

Schoonenberg, Piet. *The Christ: A Study of the God-Man Relationship in the Whole of Creation and in Jesus Christ.* New York: Herder & Herder, 1972.

Bibliography

———. *De Geest, het Woord en de Zoon*. Kampen: Kok, 1991.
Soskice, Janet. *The Kindness of God: Metaphor, Gender, and Religious Language*. Oxford: Oxford University Press, 2007.
Versteeg, Johannes P. *Christus en de Geest: Een exegetisch onderzoek naar de verhouding van de opgestane Christus en de Geest van God volgens de brieven van Paulus*. Kampen: Kok, 1971.
Villiers, Pieter G. de, ed. *The Spirit That Guides: Discernment in the Bible and Spirituality*. Bloemfontein: University of the Free State, 2013.
Vlastuin, Wim van. *Be Renewed: A Theology of Personal Renewal*. Göttingen: Vandenhoeck & Ruprecht, 2014.
Vree, Jasper, and Johan Zwaan. "Historical Introduction." In *Abraham Kuyper's Commentatio (1860): The Young Kuyper about Calvin, a Lasco, and the Church*, vol. 1: *Introduction, Annotation, Bibliography, and Indices*, edited by Jasper Vree and Johan Zwaan, 7-66. Leiden: Brill, 2005.
Waayman, Kees. "Discernment and Biblical Spirituality: An Overview and Evaluation of Recent Research." *Acta Theologica supplementum* 17 (2013): 1-12.
Warfield, Benjamin B. *Biblical and Theological Studies*, edited by Samuel S. Craig. Philadelphia: Presbyterian & Reformed, 1952.
———. *Calvin and Augustine*. Philadelphia: Presbyterian & Reformed, 1956.
———. *Calvin and Calvinism*. New York: Oxford University Press, 1931.
Weinandy, Thomas. *The Father's Spirit of Sonship: Reconceiving the Trinity*. Edinburgh: T&T Clark, 1995.
Welker, Michael. *God the Revealed: Christology*. Grand Rapids: Eerdmans, 2013.
———. *God the Spirit*. Minneapolis: Fortress, 1994.
Werner, Ilka. *Calvin und Schleiermacher im Gespräch mit der Weltweisheit: Das Verhältnis von christlichem Wahrheitsanspruch und allgemeinem Wahrheitsbewusstsein*. Neukirchen: Neukirchener Verlag, 1999.
Wolterstorff, Nicholas. *Until Justice and Peace Embrace: The Kuyper Lectures for 1981, Delivered at the Free University of Amsterdam*. Grand Rapids: Eerdmans, 1983.
Wuhrer, Helene. *Zum Stellenwert vom "Reden Gottes" im NT am Beispiel der Apostelgeschichte*. Amsterdam: VU Press, 2013.

Index of Authors

Adam, Alfred, 33
Augustine of Hippo, 72

Barnabas, Saint, 33
Barth, Karl, 5, 17, 27, 40-41,
    43, 72, 84, 89, 97, 102,
    105-6, 120, 129, 139-40
Barton, John, 36
Bauckham, Richard, 30, 41
Baur, Ferdinand C., 80
Bavinck, Herman, 12, 85, 142
Beek, Abraham van de, 97
Benedict XVI / Joseph
    Ratzinger, 43, 129
Berkhof, Hendrikus, 6-7, 39,
    46, 49-50, 55, 57
Bizer, Ernst, 12
Blumhardt, Johann Christian,
    113
Boer, Erik A., 120
Bohme, Jacob, 133
Bolt, John, 104
Bosch-Heij, Deborah van den,
    18
Bousset, Wilhelm, 40-41

Bratt, James D., 92
Brink, Gijsbert van den, 58
Buijs, Govert, 111
Busch, Eberhard, 129

Calvin, John, 72-82, 93, 99,
    101, 128
Clement of Alexandria, 34
Cocceius, Johannes, 12
Coffey, David, 29-30, 32, 44,
    46, 55-57, 69
Colle, Ralph del, 42
Congar, Yves, 7

Diederich, Martin, 82
Dingemans, Gijsbert J. D., 39
Dunn, James D. G., 9, 39, 61

Edwards, Jonathan, 72, 135

Fee, Gordon, 9
Feldmeier, Reinhard, 63
Freud, Sigmund, 133

Gaventa, Beverly R., 31, 37

Index of Authors

Grote, Geert, 81

Habets, Myk, 39
Haight, Roger, 7, 39, 46-49, 55, 57
Harnack, Adolf von, 39
Hauerwas, Stanley, 97, 121, 140
Hays, Richard, 30, 37
Hector, Kevin W., 84
Hegel, Georg W. F., 90, 140
Heppe, Heinrich von, 12
Hesselink, I. John, 79-80
Hick, John, 40
Hollenweger, Walter J., 15
Hunter, Harold, 42
Hurtado, Larry, 30, 33, 41

Ignatius of Antioch, 34

Jenson, Robert W., 42, 70
Johannes á Lasco, 90
Jüngel, Eberhard, 55, 76

Kamp, Gerrit C. van de, 33, 39
Kamphuis, Barend, 27
Keller, Tim, 140
Kooi, Cornelis van der, 32, 58, 75, 77, 102, 123
Krusche, Werner, 74
Kuyper, Abraham, 72, 78, 85, 87, 89-96, 106, 132, 139-40, 142

Lampe, Geoffrey, 7, 39
Lens, Patrick, 46, 51, 53, 62, 64-65
Lessing, Gotthold E., 36
Loofs, Friedrich, 39
Lorber, Jacob, 133

Macchia, Frank D., 106-7
Marcellus of Ancyra, 51, 54
Marthaler, Berard L., 27
Maurice, Frederick D., 72
McCormack, Bruce L., 84
McDonnell, Kilian, 7

Nevin, John W., 81
Niebuhr, H. Richard, 72, 106, 140
Norris, Kathleen, 105

Oberman, Heiko A., 80, 101
Omenyo, Cephas N., 132
Os, Bas van, 59, 134

Pannenberg, Wolfhart, 16, 27, 72
Pelikan, Jaroslav, 51
Pinnock, Clark, 7

Rahner, Karl, 7, 48, 143
Robeck, Cecil M., Jr., 15
Rothe, Richard, 140
Ruler, Arnold A. van, 72, 104, 106, 140

Sadoleto, Cardinal Jacopo, 128
Sauter, Gerhard, 36
Schlatter, Adolf, 24, 37
Schleiermacher, Friedrich D. E., 40-41, 72, 78, 82-91, 132, 140-41
Schlenke, Dorothee, 86
Scholten, J. H., 140
Schoonenberg, Piet, 30, 42, 46, 49, 51-57, 62, 64
Schweizer, Alexander, 80
Seeberg, Reinhold, 39

INDEX OF AUTHORS

Seymour, William, 15
Soskice, Janet, 61
Spieckermann, Herrmann, 63
Stanger, Friedrich, 113
Steiner, Rudolf, 133
Strauss, David Friedrich, 22
Swedenborg, Emanuel, 133

Taylor, Charles, 134
Thomas à Kempis, 81
Tillich, Paul, 7, 39

Veenhof, Jan, 7
Versteeg, Johannes P., 5-6
Villiers, Pieter G. R. de, 37-38
Vlastuin, Wim van, 15
Vree, Jasper, 90-91

Waayman, Kees, 126, 134
Warfield, Benjamin B., 9, 16, 73, 142
Weber, Max, 133
Weinandy, Thomas, 35, 42
Welker, Michael, 10, 31, 61, 86, 111, 117-18, 137, 140-41
Werner, Ilka, 82
Westphal, Joachim, 75
Wolterstorff, Nicholas, 71
Wuhrer, Helene, 37

Yoder, John H., 97, 140

Zwaan, Johan, 90-91

Index of Subjects

Acedia, 105, 139
Adoption, 77, 104, 111
American Beauty (film), 1-2, 142-43
Anointing, 24, 26, 60, 77-78, 81, 100, 107-8, 113, 124

Baptism, 109. *See also* Holy Spirit: baptism with
Beauty, 1-2
Bible, role of, 127-30
Biblical scholarship, 31-32

Cessationism, 16, 112
Charisma, 115, 123
Charismatic movements, 7, 13, 113
Christ: exaltation of, 117, 130; humanity of, 25, 33, 40, 44-45, 51; as king, 108-11, 140; as mediator, 75-76, 79; methodology of, 26-38; preexistence of, 66; threefold office of, 99-123; union with, 75, 77, 110; uniqueness of, 5, 22, 63-65, 68; vindication by, 117
Christology: anhypostasis, 23, 52; ascending and descending christology, 32, 65-66; enhypostatic union, 52-53; hypostatic union, 39, 48; Logos Christology, 23, 33, 51-54; *sessio ad dexteram*, 103; Spirit Christology, 23-24, 29-30, 33, 54; two natures Christology, 58, 101
Church, 90-91, 111; and society/culture, 91, 111, 140; as testing community, 138
Confessions/catechisms: Barmen, 131; Belgic, 43; Belhar, 131; Heidelberg, 43, 99, 104, 107, 113, 119, 130; Westminster, 43
Cosmos, 4
Councils: Chalcedon, 41, 43, 49, 67; Constantinople, 65; Second Vatican, 13, 17, 129
Creation: doctrine of, 7; as

INDEX OF SUBJECTS

mirror, 74, 80; otherness of, 11, 136; *potentia oboedientialis*, 74; slavery of, 3
Creed: Apostles', 135

Democracy, 86-87, 90-91
Discernment, 18, 36, 126-42

Ecclesiology. *See* Church
Ecumenical movement, 7, 13
Election, 92
Emptiness, 1, 8, 71, 93
Esotericism, 62, 133-34
Eucharist, 73-75, 81, 118
Extra-calvinisticum, 76, 101

Gift, 2, 73, 81, 93, 98, 105, 115
Glossolalia, 16, 122
God: counsel of, 119; doctrine of, 59, 66-69; grace of, 121; kingdom of, 88, 135; sovereignty of, 91-92; verdict of, 116
Grace, means of, 121, 123

Healing, 112; and prayer, 112-15
Holy Spirit: agency of, 37, 94, 125; avenues of, 122-23; baptism with, 106; as benevolent force/power, 2-3, 10, 12, 69-70, 74, 95, 97, 143; and church, 84, 91, 129; and eschaton, 5-6, 10, 26, 70, 81; as free self-withdrawal, 111, 137; as *Gemeingeist*, 85-86; as gift, 105; and human subjectivity, 13, 105-6; inhabitation of, 64, 104; and Jesus Christ, 10, 24, 33-34, 49-51, 60-62, 78, 93, 136; and kingdom, 88; and liberation, 10, 108, 139-40; as love, 56; as *magister interior*, 79; and novelty, 12; outpouring of, 131; and participation, 70, 76, 78, 85, 88, 103, 106, 118, 124; polyphony of, 80, 86, 121; as principle of movement, 70; *testimonium internum Spiritus Sancti*, 127-28
Holy Supper. *See* Eucharist
Hope, 140-41

Israel, 67

Jesus Christ. *See* Christ

Means of grace, 121, 123
Mission, 121, 123

(Neo-)Calvinism, 8, 71, 85

Office, threefold, 99-123; kingly dimension of, 107-15; priestly dimension of, 115-19; prophetic dimension of, 119-23, 133

Participation. *See* Holy Spirit: and participation
Pentecostal movement, 7, 13, 121, 126, 130
Person, 53
Pneuma-theology, 7
Pneumatology, 1-21; renewal movements and, 17-18; rise of, 6-17. *See also* Holy Spirit
Prophecy, 122, 132

Index of Subjects

Reconciliation, 117-18
Reformed tradition/spirituality, 15, 17-18, 81, 122-23, 127-29
Regeneration, 95
Revelation, 48-49, 132

Sacrament, 73, 80, 121
Salvation, 14, 18
Salvation history, 102
Society: as organism, 87, 90; and transformation, 72, 111, 119, 142
Spirit, Holy. *See* Holy Spirit
Spirit, human, 82-83, 136
Symbol, 47, 49

Testimonium internum Spiritus Sancti, 127-28
Theology, Trinitarian, 7-9, 29, 51, 57; key functions of, 19-21; missional and return model, 30, 32, 50, 69
Transformation, 71-76, 81-89, 93, 106, 111, 141-43

"Ugly ditch" (Lessing), 36

Witness, 120-21
Word and Spirit, 79, 120, 126-29

Xenolalia, 123

Index of Scripture References

OLD TESTAMENT

Genesis
6:3 — 10

Exodus
15:8–10 — 10

Deuteronomy
18:22 — 137

Judges
3:10 — 10
6:34 — 10
11:29 — 10
16:20 — 10

1 Samuel
8:4–9 — 110
10:10–11 — 10
19:23–24 — 10

Job
26:12–13 — 10
33:4 — 10

Psalms
18:5 — 10
24:1 — 125
25 — 127
36:9b — 139
72 — 110

Proverbs
8 — 68

Ecclesiastes
9:7–9 — 2

Isaiah — 10
32:15–16 — 11
34:16 — 11
40:6–7 — 10
57:16 — 11
61 — 120, 141

Jeremiah
28 — 138

Ezekiel — 10
2:2 — 11

3:14 — 11
11:5 — 11

NEW TESTAMENT

Matthew
1:18–25 — 56
1:23 — 22
4:1 — 25
5:13 — 72
11:3 — 139
11:3–5 — 25
11:4–5 — 141
11:27 — 60, 63
25:31–46 — 126
26:39 — 33

Mark
1:12 — 25
1:21–28 — 108
3:7–12 — 60
14:36 — 33
14:62 — 108

Index of Scripture References

Luke
1:26–38   56
2:40   33
4:1–2   25
4:14–30   120
4:19   120
10:25–37   111

John
1:1   23, 64, 67
5:1–15   118
6:35   64
6:38   60
8:28–29   60
8:58   64
10   126
16:12–14   37
16:13   20, 28
17   68
19:21   108

Acts
2   123
2:17–18   131
5:38–39   138
10–11   37
10:15   37
10:37–38   24
10:38   61, 102
11:28   138

Romans
5:5   125
8:3   63
8:20–21   3
8:29   46
8:32   63
12:1   117

1 Corinthians
8:6   67–68
14:2   122

2 Corinthians
1:19–20   102
3:17a   50
3:18   106
5:19–20   118

Ephesians
1:4   67
4:20–24   106

Philippians
2:5–11   30
3:12–14   106
4:8   140

Colossians
1:16   67

1 Timothy
3:16   3

2 Timothy
4:1   126

Hebrews
5:1–9   25
5:8   33
12:2   44

1 Peter
2:9   122

2 Peter
3:13   5

Revelation
5:5–7   117
12:10   126

www.ingramcontent.com/pod-product-compliance
Lightning Source LLC
Chambersburg PA
CBHW031314150426
43191CB00005B/226